Glenn & Sue Hawks
930 Fairview Road
Ojai, California 93023

Muhammad, Judah & Joseph Smith

Muhammad, Judah & Joseph Smith

by
C. Reynolds MacKay

BONNEVILLE BOOKS™
Springville, Utah

ISBN: 1-55517-624-0
e.1

Published by Bonneville Books
Imprint of Cedar Fort Inc.
www.cedarfort.com

Distributed by:

Typeset by Kristin Nelson
Cover design by Adam Ford
Cover design © 2002 by Lyle Mortimer

Printed in the United States of America
10 9 8 7 6 5 4 3 2 1

Printed on acid-free paper

Library of Congress Cataloging-in-Publication Data

MacKay, C. Reynolds.
  Muhammad, Judah & Joseph Smith / by C. Reynolds MacKay.
     p. cm.
Includes bibliographical references and index.
  ISBN 1-55517-624-0 (pbk. : alk. paper)
  1. Religions. 2. Islam. 3. Judaism. 4. Mormon Church. I. Title:
Muhammad, Judah, and Joseph Smith. II. Title.
  BL85 .M189 2002
  291--dc21
                           2002010065

iv

CONTENTS

GLOSSARY

CALIPH—Successor to Muhammad as head of the Sunni Muslims. The Sunnis consist of 85 percent of Muslims, the Shiites, 15 percent. The Caliphate in Turkey was abolished in 1924.

DHIMMI—Nonbelievers, such as Jews, Christians, and Zoroastrians who live in Muslim countries under Islamic law.

DAR-AL-ISLAM—Territory ruled by Islam.

DAR-AL-HARB—Territory ruled by non Muslims

HADITHS—Muslim traditions. Sayings of Muhammad and Imans. Second only to the Koran as the most holy of Islam books.

HAJJ—The pilgrimage to Mecca required by all Muslims at least once in their lives.

IMAN—Religious leader. Among the Twelver Shiites, one of the twelve legitimate successors to Muhammad.

ISLAM—Submission to God from Aslama—*he surrendered* (American Heritage Dictionary of the English Language). Semitic root, to be whole. Arabic *salama*, he was safe and at peace. Hebrew shalom, peace. Greek salome, peace.

JIHAD—Holy war to expand Islam.

KAFIR—Infidels who have rejected Islam.

MADRASA—Religious school where Islamic sciences are taught, including the rightness of Jihad. Funded especially by Saudi Arabia.

MAHDI—The Messiah waited for by Shiites, especially the Twelfth Iman, who is at present unseen.

MUFTI—Religious leader who interprets Muslim law.

MUJAHIDIN—Muslim warrior engaged in a holy war.

SEMITE—Chiefly of caucasian stock comprising Jews and Arabs, but in ancient times including Babylonians, Assyrians, and others of the eastern Mediterranean area. Subfamily of afro-Asiatic family of languages, including Arabic, Hebrew, and Aramaic. Descendants of Shem. (American Heritage Dictionary of the English Language). SHARIA. Koranic and Hadith laws.

SUFISM—Muslim mysticism. Attracts some American converts.

SURA—One of the 114 chapters of the Koran.

ULAMA—A Muslim who is learned.

PREFACE

Islam along with Judaism and Christianity traces its origin back to Abraham. Beginning in the seventh century, 650 years after Christianity and 2000 years after Judaism, Islam has grown to be the religion of 20-25 percent of the world's population. Fifteen percent of Muslims are Shiites, claiming direct descendants from Fatima, Muhammad's daughter and Ali, his adopted son. The rest are Sunnis, who came from leaders who surrounded Muhammad and formed the Caliph or leader, a position persisting until it ended in 1924 in Turkey.

Islam during the Dark Ages is represented by Persia, where great art, poetry, architecture, science, and astronomy were outstanding. At the same time, Europe was wallowing with scandals in the dominant Catholic Church, where selling of indulgences and clashing feudal kingdoms were ubiquitous.

The Catholic hierarchy insisted that the sun and planets evolved around the earth, and scientists who disagreed were in danger of death or prison. After the Magna Carta and the fall of Constantinople, Christianity has been constantly advancing. Christianity has been favorable to scientific progress while Islam has undergone a *volte face*.

Sufis, the mystics of Islam, contributed much to the spread of Islam. One of the greatest Sufi saints was Abd-al-Quadr-Jilani (1077-1160) who preached in Baghdad. His tenets, which have received acclaim, are the following:

1. Never swear by God. Never use the Lord's name.

2. Never speak an untruth.

3. Never swear at anyone.

4. Never break a promise.

ix

5. Never accuse someone of religious infidelity.

6. Never be a party to anything sinful.

7. Never harm anyone.

8. Never accept anything from others. God alone is the giver.

9. Never impose a burden on others.

10. Look for good in others, rather than the bad.

Muhammad's Farewell Address:

1. All Muslims are brethren unto one another. They are equal in every respect.

2. An Arab has no superiority over a non-Arab, or non-Arab over an Arab.

3. A white man does not possess any superiority over a black man nor a black man over a white man, except in point of piety.

Hopefully, modern Muslims will accept these admonitions and philosophies and bring peace to our world, which is on the brink of disastrous conflict between good and evil, slavery and freedom, hate and friendship. Never before has the line been drawn so clearly between Satanic efforts of fundamental radical Muslims who want to destroy the way of life of all free men and the inalienable rights endowed them by their Creator.

INTRODUCTION

Islam means submission to God, from the Arabic *salama*. Islam has spread around the world and is claimed to be the fastest growing religion in the United States.

The conflict between those who insist on strict adherence to the Koran and Sharia, the Islamic law of medieval times, continues against modernistic muslims who want progress and more tolerant behavior.

The Jihad or holy war has existed since Muhammad, and recently has reared its ugly head in the terrorism attacks around the world. They have struck at American embassies in Africa, the World Trade Center, and the U.S.S. Cole in Yemen. They also successfully assassinated Sadat. They continue attempts to overthrow the government of Egypt and other nations where moderate Islamic regimes exist.

Israel, the only democratic country in the Middle East has suffered terrorist attacks by the Hamas and radical Palestinians for years.

According to the State Department report—known as the International Religious Freedom Act of 1998—religious persecution persists in twenty states where Islam is the dominant religion.

Our ally, Pakistan, has been urged by our government to overturn their law stipulating the death penalty or life in prison for speaking pejoratively about Muhammad.

Freedom of religion does not exist in Indonesia or in Saudi Arabia, where a Muslim apostate is subject to death by beheading.

In Algeria and Nigeria, violent civil war has raged to eliminate Jews and Christians, massacring thousands. In the Philippines, with ties to Al Qaeda, Muslims are trying to form an independent southern Islamic state. Colin Powell has called Sudan the most egregious and despicable country in the world concerning Human Rights.

Islam has always shown hatred of atheists, pagans, Hindus, Sikhs, Zoroastrians, Jews, Buddhists, and Christians, *despite some parts of the Koran which plead for tolerance.*

Usama bin Laden ordered the bombing of the American embassies in Nairobi, Kenya, and Tanzania. Two hundred people were killed and 5,000 injured. In February 1998, Usama bin Laden ordered Muslims to kill Americans, likening Americans to ancient Crusaders. On September 11, 2001, terrorism exploded inside the borders of the United States.

Kate O'Beirne, in her excellent article, "Muslim Murder and Mayhem Against Christians," in *National Review*, December 3, 2001, identifies the continuing Islamic Jihad. She points out that in the *Wall Street Journal* recently, journalist Amir Taheri noted that twenty-eight of the thirty active conflicts in the world involve Muslim communities or governments.

O'Bierne notes that in *The Clash of Civilizations and the Remaking of World Order,* Samuel P. Huntington writes, "Wherever one looks along the perimeter of Islam, Muslims have problems living peaceably with their neighbors . . . And in the 1990s they have been far more involved in intergroup violence than the people of any other civilization."

As O'Bierne further notes, Huntington argues that Islamic militancy is not an aberrant strain, but an endemic part of Islam: "The underlying problem for the West is not Islamic fundamentalism. It is Islam, a different civilization whose people are convinced of the superiority of their culture and are obsessed with the inferiority of their power."

Writing in 1996, Huntington says: "Some Westerners including President Bill Clinton, have argued that the West does not have problems with Islam but only with violent Islamist extremists. Fourteen hundred years of history demonstrate otherwise."

Most American Muslims love the United States' economy, and they try to enjoy the American Dream. Their religion doesn't prevent them from doing all they can to acquire vast wealth, much like Sikhs in Arabia. Muslims in America have expressed hatred against Jews and Americans and have even advocated a separate state, or Nation of Islam, a Balkanization of America.

Islam believes that it has not only a superior culture, but that their destiny of dominating the world is the will of God.

Islamic-dominated countries must decide whether they will allow freedom, democracy, and tolerance to exist, or plunge our planet back into dark and evil times where freedom is disallowed.

Chapter 1

THE PROPHET MUHAMMAD

Muhammad was born in 570 AD in Mecca, Saudi Arabia. His father died a few months before he was born and his mother died when he was six. He was raised by his grandfather. When his grandfather died two years later, he was taken in by his uncle. His cousin, Ali, became like a brother to Muhammad.

When he was twenty-five, Muhammad married Khadija, who was fifteen years his senior, and took no other wives as long as she lived. They had eight children, but only four daughters grew to adulthood. Muhammad also took his cousin Ali into his household, along with a freed slave, Zayd.

After his wife died, Muhammad acquired a Harem of a dozen wives and concubines. At the age of forty Muhammad claimed that the Angel Gabriel appeared to him, dictated the Koran to him (Muhammad could neither read nor write, although this is disputed by historians and some Muslim religious leaders) on behalf of Allah, and told Muhammad he was a Prophet of God. Thus, Muhammad founded Islam.

At that time in Arabia people were paganistic and worshiped idols. It has been recorded that in Mecca there were three hundred idols. These deities were worshiped in the holy meccan site of the Kaaba, the site of a large stone. Every year people came to worship at the Kaaba and walk around it seven times. These visitors brought a lot of money to the businessmen of Mecca, and when Muhammad claimed the idols were worthless and he confirmed the Jewish and Christian belief that there is only one true God, fear of losing their income inflamed the Meccans, and they forced Muhammad to move to Medina.

According to Malise Ruthven: "The Muhammad who is lodged in the Muslim psyche is not the same as the Muhammad of history." The war with the Meccans occurred at Badr in 623 when Muhammad defeated them soundly in battle, aided according to Muhammad, by 5,000 angels with Gabriel at the head. Only Muhammad saw the angels.

According to history, during one twenty-four-hour period, Muhammad arrested six hundred captive Jews of the Beni Quoraiga tribe in Medina, who had opposed him and beheaded them. The slaughter resulted in obtaining slaves, livestock, land, jewelry, and money, which was divided, with one fifth going to the prophet. This is recorded in the Koran (11:25): "*God helped the faithful in the stress of war: mighty is God, and all-powerful. He brought down from their strongholds those who had supported Him from the People of the Book (Jews of Beni Quoraiga) and cast terror into their hearts, so that some you slew and others you took captive. He made you masters of their land, their houses, and their goods.*"

Muslims must accept every word of the Koran and claim it came from God through Gabriel. Muhammad dictated the messages to his slave secretary, Zayd, who wrote it down on parchment and stones. It was later written in book form in Arabic.

Islams accept Abraham, Noah, Isaac, Ishmael, Jacob, Moses, Joseph, and Jesus as prophets, and claim that Muhammad is the last prophet and there will be no more. The prophet interprets the word of God in the form of teaching and laws. According to Traditions (Hadiths) of Muslims there have been 144,000 prophets, with Abraham the chief Prophet, followed by well known prophets in the Scriptures, including Jesus.

According to the historian John Keegan, Muhammad, unlike Christ, was a man of violence. He bore arms, was wounded in battle, and preached holy war, or Jihad, against those who defied the will of God as revealed to him, Muhammad. He said, "The sword is the key to heaven and hell." This is the opposite of Christ's admonition, who said, "He who lives by the sword shall die by the sword."

Muhammad ordered the assassination of his foes. The Koran says, "When you meet the unbelievers, strike off their heads until you have massacred them. Fight in the cause of Allah. Kill them wherever you find them."

By 656 A.D., the first three caliphs, followers of Muhammad, were murdered (Umar, Ali, and Othman). Turkey abolished the caliphate in 1924, became a secular republic, and has become a staunch U.S. Ally.

THE HADITH

In addition to the Koran is the *Hadith* or *Traditions*, consisting of sayings and rules made by the Prophet, gathered by his followers a hundred years after his death. Al-Bukari, (al-Bukari, Ed. L.K. Krehl, 4 vols., E.J.Brill, Leiden, 1862), an early writer of Islam, accepted only 7,275 of the 600,000 stories about Muhammad, which he called *The Correct Book*, which were added to the *Hadith*.

> *"He (God) replied: 'I will visit My scourge upon whom I please. Those that shall follow the Apostle—the Unlettered Prophet—described to them in the Torah and the Gospel, he will enjoin righteousness upon them and forbid them to do evil"* (K 7:157).
>
> *"Never have you (Muhammad) read a book before this, nor have you ever transcribed one with your right hand"* (K 29:46).

Muslims may claim Muhammad was unable to read or write, but he and his scribes were apparently very learned in the scriptures.

Muslims claim that Islam teaches only one interpretation of the Koran, but, as pointed out by Hugh Nibley, "One of the most famous *Hadiths* or sayings attributed to Muhammad is that 'There are seventy seven sects in Islam (already in his day) and all but one are for the burning."

Again from Nibley, "The Koran claims to be the complete and final word of God, yet the doctors of Islam have handed down tens of thousands of *Hadiths*, that is, things Muhammad is reported to have said."

Undoubtedly, Muhammad was highly intelligent and charismatic. He was courageous, and a typical medieval warrior. He was faithful to his first wife, and acquired a harem only after her death.

He began life as an orphan, worked hard as a youth and claimed to receive a vision from the angel Gabriel, becoming a Prophet of God. He founded a religion which embodies a fifth of the world's population, and intends to become the dominant power in the world, forcing the world to adhere to its religious views and laws.

Muslim Mongols and Ottoman warriors struck fear into the hearts of the world, conquering much of Europe and Asia. Today, Islamic mujhadins again hope to repeat the success of previous times by terrorist tactics. They justify their atrocities by claiming it to be the will of God and will use anything in their power, whether it be hijacked airplanes, bomb carriers bent on suicide, poisoning water supplies in urban cities, spreading plague-producing organisms or radio-active materials, or, if possible, atom bomb-laden missiles.

Chapter 2

MUSLIM VERSUS MUSLIM

After the death of Muhammad a group of notables of Islam elected Abu Bakr to be the caliph or successor to Muhammad. Ali, who became the son-in-law of Muhammad was considered to be the rightful successor, not only because he was Muhammad's secretary and constantly at his side, but because Muhammad at one time put his arm around Ali and said, "This is my brother and successor." Shiites thus believe that Ali was not only to be temporal head (Caliph) but also spiritual head (Imam).

The successor (Caliph) to Muhammad was Abu Bakr, who was ambitious. Bakr was succeeded by Umar and Uthman, by 656 the Caliphate had invaded the Arabian peninsula, Palestine, Syria, Egypt, Libya, Mesopotamia and parts of Armenia and Persia. Following the assassination of Uthman, Ali assumed the leadership. When Ali was assassinated, the Shiites refused to recognize the governor of Syria, and the new Caliphi, Muawiya, made Damascus the capital and conquered Tunisia. Muslim forces reached into North Africa in 710, overran Spain, and reached into France. Muawiya was a great military leader.

Turkish Muslims seized Baghdad in 1055 and defeated the Byzantines in 1071, precipitating the crusades. Two great Islamic powers emerged, the Ottomans and the Monguls. The Ottomans conquered Constantinople, and the Ottoman empire extended into vast areas of Europe.

Islam spread into Java, Indonesia, the Philippines, Russia, and Africa. Today there are 140 million Muslims in Indonesia, 85 percent of the population.

The Imams or spiritual leaders are believed by Islams to be assisted by God through the Holy Spirit. The third Imam, Husayn, was asked, "From where do you get your authority?" He replied, "We rule by the House of David, and if we lack anything then the Holy Spirit sends it to us." (In Introduction to Shi`I Islam, Moojan Momen, George Ronald Publisher, Oxford, 1985).

At one time in history Shiites believed in an anthropomorphic God, but later this was dropped. In modern times the dominance of modern Shiite doctrine has been seen in the era of the Ayatollah Khomeni, who believed that Islam is not just an ethical religion but has all the laws and principles necessary for government and social administration, and he invoked the Koran and Traditions as the constitution of Iran and enforced its rules.

Shiite law allows temporary marriage, while Sunni does not.

The assassination of Ali provided the Shiites a martyr, and their hatred of the Sunnis continues even today. Omar Quadhaphi of Libya denigrated Muhammad, almost claiming to be a new prophet. He said, "What has Muhammad done that I have not? It is I who liberated you and gave you international standing."

Vicious wars have been fought between muslims and between Islamic nations. One of the most notable was the war between Iran, consisting of mostly Shiites, and Iraq, predominantly Sunni. Each claimed to be supported by Allah. It was one Jihad against the other.

The Koran specifically forbids wars between Muslims: *"It is unlawful for a believer to kill another believer. He that kills a believer by design shall burn in hell forever"* (K 4:93).

Chapter 3

THE ISLAM MESSIAH

The Mahdi, the Islam Messiah, is to return at the end of the world to restore peace and righteousness. Shiite Muslims believe he is the twelfth Imam, who is occult or invisible. Most Shiites belong to the "Twelvers."

The "Twelvers" believe the following:

1. The Mahdi will be a descendant of the Prophet Muhammad through his daughter, Fatima.
2. Before the Mahdi comes there will be the red death (the sword) and the white death (the plague).
3. The sun will rise from the West and a star will rise in the East.
4. Arabs will take over their land, throwing out the foreigners.
5. Syria will be destroyed after a conflict.
6. Death and fear will occur in Iraq. A fire will appear in the sky.
7. The Mahdi will come with a new book and a new law.
8. The Anti-Christ will appear in the East. Christ will return.

Chapter 4

ISLAM IN EVERY-DAY LIFE

In addition to praying three times a day in a prostrate position, the religion of Islam governs many aspects of living. It gives details of toilet, bath, greeting, table manners , and even the most minor and private matters such as defecation, brushing teeth, sleeping, prayers, and sexual activities. It is very ritualistic, much as ancient and some modern orthodox Judaism.

During the Ayatollah Khomeni's reign, strict Shiite rules were re-imposed—including veils for women, strict control of the state by Islam, laws based on the Koran, and a return to Jihad. Fortunately, today Iran is ruled by more moderate rulers. Iran has made great strides in modernizing its country, including technology.

H.G. Wells said: "Islam prevailed because it was the best social and political order the times had to offer. It prevailed because everywhere it found politically apathetic people, robbed, oppressed, bullied, uneducated. It offered better terms than any others to the masses."

The Sufis and Dervish often appealed to people by their ritualistic and spiritual activities. The "Holy Rollers" of Christian sects have similar attraction.

Professor T.W. Arnold claimed that among the most powerful factors at work in the production of stupendous results in the spread of Islam over the globe were Muslim Missionaries: "The Muslim warrior had a sword in one hand and the Koran in the other."

"Blessed are the believers who are humble in their prayers; who avoid profane talk, and give alms to the destitute; who restrain their carnal desires (except with their wives and slave girls)" (K 25:1).

Chapter 5

OILY JIHAD

The discovery of oil in the Middle East changed the whole dynamics of Islamic world politics and power. Israelis complain that "Moses wandered around for forty years and settled in Israel, the only place in the the Middle East where there was no oil."

Oil makes the Christian West obsequious to the Muslim East. Muslims accept oil as a gift of God.

The Sheiks and monarchs of Saudi Arabia have used oil to build great modern cities and enjoy their wealth. They used American know-how to develop their vast resources and refineries, then nationalized them. They helped form OPEC to control the world market. Saudis finance Islamic groups surreptitiously. The ten billion dollars Saudi gives in foreign aid goes 99 percent to Muslims in the rest of the world to promote Sharia, Islamic law.

The king of Saudi Arabia said, "The main resource to depend upon is oil." Some accuse Saudi Arabia for directing the overthrow of Bhutto of Pakistan, and replace him with a more strict Muslim. Musharraf, prime minister of Pakistan, has withstood the efforts of extremists and has supported the West in the war against terrorists.

Unknown to most Americans, Saudi Arabia provides more than one billion dollars to the PLO (Time, July 18, 1992).

Radical terrorist groups have tried to overthrow the government of Egypt and have tried several times to assassinate Mubarak, as they did Anwar Sadat. Sadat and Mubarak have both tried to modernize Egypt and allow some freedoms of its people, despite the efforts of extremists to impose strict intolerant Muslim laws and practices.

France sold arms and nuclear installations in Iraq for oil contracts, and the United States held back on filling strategic oil reserves in deference to Saudi Arabia. Politicians in Japan and Europe have made anti-Israel statements to please Arabic oil exporters.

Quadhafi has trained saboteurs, sponsored terrorism and called for revolution in Saudi Arabia to overthrow the monarchy.

The United States has become dependent on the oil of Saudi Arabia, with over 40 percent coming from that country or other OPEC nations. This dependence hinders our efforts to force Arabia to change its strict Islam laws, and allow people civil rights. Saudi Arabia does not allow any other religion in the country, and has not stopped exporting money for terrorism. The hijackers who crashed into the World Trade Center were Saudi nationalists.

To its peril, the United States continues to be hostage to Muslim countries for our oil. Oil is fuelling the continuing Jihad against the West, and we continue to supply the cash in knee jerk response.

Chapter 6

THE CRUSADES AND COLONIALISM

Muslims and historians continue to blame the Crusades as the beginning of conflict between Islam and Christianity, despite the fact that Islamic Jihad and the spread of Islamic religion and law had been going on 400 years before the Crusades, beginning with Muhammad. The Crusades lasted just 200 years while the Jihad has never stopped.

In 1998 Usama bin Laden called his terrorist group the "International Islamic Front for Jihad Against Jews and Christian Crusaders." Fortunately many Muslim leaders decry terrorism, and deny that the Koran and the Jihad apply to today's modern enlightened world.

Crusaders, like Mujhadeens, were often cruel, brutal, and ruthless. They often declared war in the name of Christianity, but did not follow the admonition of Christ to "Love your enemies. Do good to those that spitefully use you."

Many books have been written denouncing the Crusaders who were bent on recovering Jerusalem—previously held Byzantine territory—from the Muslim hordes which had swept across the Holy Land, Southern Europe, the Balkans, and Spain. As noted by Paul Fregosi in his book, *Jihad*, little has been written about the Jihad and vast colonization by the Muslims.

The Crusades were fought by some who wanted financial gain and prestige. However, most had religious aims, not just materialistic aims. Many were wealthy landlords who had little to gain and everything to lose by joining the Crusades. It is true that many of the Crusaders were brutal, which was typical of warriors in medieval times.

As pointed out by Fregosi, Muslim Jihad against the West was held in check for centuries during the colonization of Arabic nations by Britain, France, the Netherlands, Spain and Italy. After World War II they regained their independence and sovereignty. Aided by the riches of oil, Muslim-controlled nations emerged, and immigration to the West as well as to the rest of the world by Muslims occurred in great numbers.

Again, as noted by Fregosi in his excellent book, *Jihad*—although colonization of Muslim countries by nations such as England, France, and Germany lasted about 200 years—the colonization of many countries in Europe by Muslims lasted much longer, from 660 A.D. to 1950. Muhammad organized 65 military campaigns, and, following his death, Muslim conquerors spread over the Middle East, Northern Africa, the Balkans, southern Europe, Russia, Indonesia, the Philippines, and made inroads into France, Spain, Portugal, France, and the Byzantine Empire. Muslims occupied Spain 400 years, Portugal 600 years, Sicily 300 years, Greece 500 years, Bulgaria 500, Hungary 150, Rumania 400, and Serbia 400 years. In America today, it is estimated that there are two million Muslims, not just from immigration, but by conversion, especially among the blacks.

Chapter 7

THE PROPHET JOSEPH SMITH

Detractors of the Mormon church (The Church of Jesus Christ of Latter-day Saints) claim that it is not a Christian church and claim it has substituted the Book of Mormon for the Bible, despite the fact that Mormons constantly read the scriptures, believing the Bible to be the word of God as long as it is translated correctly.

Neal A. Maxwell, an LDS Church apostle, points out that many deny the Book of Mormon without ever having read it. From its beginning with six members in 1830 the church has grown to over 11 million, with more members outside the United States than within, and the Book of Mormon has been translated into most foreign languages.

Joseph Smith, who, at the age of fifteen was confused by all the claims of various religious sects, read in James 1:5 that God would answer prayer to any who lack wisdom and who asked with unwavering faith. The Smith boy went into the woods and knelt in prayer and saw two heavenly personages, one of whom said, pointing to the other, "This is my Beloved Son. Hear Him."

Christ then told Joseph in answer to his query, that no church on earth was the one true church, that "They speak of me with their lips, but their hearts are far from me."

Later, Joseph Smith was visited by an angel named Moroni who informed him that he would find in a local hill a book of golden plates written in ancient Egyptian about a group of people who emigrated to the Americas from Jerusalem 600 years before the birth of Christ. Moroni told Smith that he would be able to translate the book with the help of a Urim and Thummim, similar to that device mentioned in the Old Testament. It was three years later that Joseph Smith was allowed to recover the plates of gold and begin to translate them, which became known as the Book of Mormon.

The boy Joseph was amazed at the furor he caused, when, as an unlearned boy, he claimed to have an answer to his prayer and saw the glorious personages of the Father and the Son. He said, "I have told the truth. I saw God the Father and Jesus Christ. I know that I saw them; God knows that I know it—and I cannot deny it, or I will receive the wrath of God."

Joseph Smith said, "It was nevertheless a fact that I had beheld a vision. I have thought since, that I felt much like Paul, when he went before King Agrippa, and related the account of the vision he had when he saw a light, and heard a voice—but there were few who believed him.

"Some said Paul was dishonest, others said he was mad, and he was ridiculed and reviled. But all this did not destroy the reality of his vision. He had seen a vision, he knew he had, and all the persecution under heaven could not make it otherwise, though they should persecute him unto death.

"So it was with me. I had actually seen a light, and in the midst of that light I saw two personages, and they did in reality speak to me, and though I was hated and persecuted for saying that I had seen a vision, yet it was true. And while they were persecuting me, reviling me, and speaking all manner of evil against me falsely for so saying, I was led to say in my heart: "Why persecute me for telling the truth. I have actually seen a vision, and who am I that I can withstand God, or why does the world think to make me deny what I have actually seen. For I had seen a vision; I knew it, and I knew that God knew it, and I could not deny it."

TEACHINGS OF THE PROPHET JOSEPH SMITH:

1. No man is saved faster than he gets knowledge. Add to knowledge virtue and to virtue faith.

2. "The Mormons will become a mighty people in the midst of the Rocky Mountains." At the time, the Mormons were in Nauvoo, Illinois, and planned on staying there. They had built the city on the banks of the Missouri river and turned it into one of the largest cities west of St. Louis.

3. A prophet is only a prophet when he is acting like one.

4. Professors of religion who do not believe in revelations, which were continued to be given to Christ's church down through the ages, will be damned.

8. We don't ask people to throw away any good they have, we only ask them to come and get more.

9. We will obtain knowledge a little at a time—then we can comprehend it.

10. The word Mormon means "more good," and does not come from the Greek or Latin. There was no Greek or Latin on the plates, which I, through the grace of God, translated. The Book of Mormon was written in reformed Egyptian.

11. Compare the principle of prophesy and revelation with the Christendom of present day—with all the boasted religion, piety, and sacredness, while at the same time crying out against prophesy and continuous revelation. Religions reject the most glorious principles of the gospel of Jesus Christ.

12. The great principle of Mormonism is to receive truth— let it come when and where it may.

13. I will not try to compel any person to believe as I do, except by the force of reasoning, for truth will work its own way.

14. Is exaltation possible without all the ordinances? The answer is no. Any person exalted to the highest kingdom must obey the celestial laws.

15. *God Himself was once as we are now and dwelt on an earth just as we do. Jesus was asked what He was going to do and replied that He was going to lay down His life as His Father did, and take it up again* (John 5:19).

16. You must learn to be gods yourself—going from the small degree to another. When you climb a ladder, you must begin at the bottom and ascend step by step. You must begin with the first one and go until you learn all the steps of exaltation.

17. The difference between the Mormon and other churches is that we have the Holy Ghost by which is meant that the power of the Holy Ghost and the will of our Father in Heaven and Jesus Christ is given to the leaders of our church through the Holy Ghost.

18. Marriage sealed by the Holy Spirit is eternal. Until death do we part is abolished and the family unit continues forever.

19. Our perfection depends upon doing vicarious rituals for the dead. The dead cannot be made perfect without us, who perform baptism for the dead and other necessary physical acts for them.

20. The testimony of Jesus is the spirit of prophesy and anyone who says he is teaching righteousness and denies the spirit of prophesy is a liar, and, thus, false teachers and imposters may be detected.

21. The United States was prepared to be the place for the restoration of the true Gospel of Jesus Christ, and America will never be destroyed, provided it remains righteous.

22. Many false prophets have arisen, and more will come and deceive many.

23. The Lord has said, "You shall defend your families even unto bloodshed."

24. When Joseph Smith asked the Lord which church he should join he was told to joint none of them for "Though they have a form of godliness, the power of godliness they shun. They draw near me with their lips but their hearts are far away. They teach the doctrines of men and stray from God."

25. The Church of Jesus Christ of Latter-day Saints is like an impenetrable, immovable rock in the midst of the mighty deep, exposed to the storms and tempests of Satan. We hope he will continue to stir up the sink of iniquity, that the people more readily discern between the righteous and the wicked.

26. If there is anything in the Bible which does not authorize the belief in modern revelation, we have not been able to find it.

27. If the canon of scriptures were full, the scriptures would have said so. The Book of Revelations has reference only to that book written by Paul, not the Bible as a whole, inasmuch as other books were written after Revelations.

28. The Book of Mormon, like the Bible, has references to other books which have been lost, or will be revealed later. The Book of Mormon and the Doctrine and Covenants may have other scriptures or books added to them.

29. "I have constantly said that no man shall have more than one wife at a time, unless the Lord directs otherwise."

30. We have endeavored to teach the fulness of the Gospel of Jesus Christ. Those who have borne false witness against us may kill our bodies, but never our souls.

31. If anyone should ask me if I were a prophet, I should not deny it. For, according to John, the testimony of Jesus is the spirit of prophesy. Any person who declares he is a prophet and denies the spirit of the Holy Ghost is a liar.

32. As well might a man stretch forth his puny arm to stop the Missouri river or turn it upstream as to hinder the Almighty from pouring down knowledge from heaven upon the heads of the Latter Day Saints.

33. Mormonism is truth. God is its author. It was from God that we received the Book of Mormon.

34. Daily transgressions with daily repentance does not please God.

35. Faith comes not by signs, but by hearing and believing the word of God.

36. No person can be called to any office in the Church without the gift of the Holy Ghost.

37. Attempts to promote peace and happiness in the human family have proved abortive. Every effort throughout history has failed. Peace and happiness need the wisdom of God, the intelligence of God, and the power of God.

38. The earth is groaning under corruption, oppression, tyranny and bloodshed and the Lord is coming out of his hiding place.

38. Many of the righteous shall fall prey to disease and pestilence and yet be saved in the kingdom of God.

39. Satan has power over us only as we allow it.

40. God set the sun and planets and stars in the heavens with certain laws which they cannot break. Every plant, tree and seed shall bring forth its kind and cannot come forth under any other law.

41. Everyone shall come from the grave and be raised by the

power of God. (Universal Resurrection).

42. While people cherish honor and support knaves, hypocrites, and imposters, the earth banished prophets as vagabonds.

43. Neither Jew nor heathen can be culpable if they haven't heard the truth. They will have the opportunity to believe or reject the truth in the hereafter. The priesthood not only administers on earth, but also in heaven, in order that people might fulfill all the requirements of God."

44. All people must endure affliction and tribulation to prove themselves, just as Jesus had to endure affliction to prove Himself.

45. God has created men and women with an intellect, and the more learning they acquire the greater will be their joy. The closer they get to God, the less they want to sin.

46. The first principle of the Gospel is to know for a certainty the character of God, and know that we might converse with Him as one person converses with another; to know that He was a person like us; to know that God the Father dwelt on an earth and experienced mortal life like we have and as did His Son Jesus Christ.

47. The Book of Mormon is the most correct of any book on earth and the keystone of our religion. A person would get nearer to God by abiding by its precepts than any other book.

48. It is quite necessary for you to be tried as it was with Abraham. God will take hold of you and wrench your very heartstrings, and if you can't stand it you will not be fit for the Celestial kingdom of God.

49. God is in the form of man, with a striking resemblance to Jesus Christ.

A BIBLE! A BIBLE!

"Many of the Gentiles shall say: 'A Bible, A Bible! We have got a Bible' . . . what thank they the Jews for the Bible which they receive from them? . . . have ye remembered the Jews, mine ancient covenant people? Nay, but ye have cursed them and have hated them . . . Have ye obtained a Bible save it were by the Jews? Know ye not that there are more nations than one? . . . I speak the same words unto one nation like unto another . . . [to] prove . . . that I am the same yesterday, today, and forever.

"For I shall speak unto the Jews and they shall write it; and I shall speak unto the other tribes of the house of Israel. The Jews shall have the words of the Nephites and the Nephites shall have the words of the Jews. And my people, which are of the house of Israel shall be gathered home, and I will show unto them that fight against my word and against my people, who are of the house of Israel, that I am God, and that I covenanted with Abraham that I would remember his seed forever (2 Nephi 29).

This is the only true and living church upon the face of the earth, which I the Lord am well pleased (Doctrine and Covenants 1:30).

You shall know that I lie not; for you shall see me at the bar of God. The Lord will say to you, Did I not declare my words to you, which were written by this man, like one crying from the dead, even as one speaking out of the dust? (Moroni 10:27).

"We are not perfect. While the church was organized under divine guidance, we fall short of our ideals, but with the additional revelations from the Lord and with the gift of the Holy Ghost, we hope it may be said of the Latter-day Saints what Peter said of former day Saints: "Ye are a chosen generation, a royal priesthood, a holy nation, a peculiar people, that you should show forth the praises of Him who called you out of darkness into a marvelous light" (Hugh B. Brown, church apostle, 1958).

"The men of Sodom called unto Lot and told him to bring the two men out to him that they might know them. Lot said, I have two daughters which are virgins. I pray, bring them out and abuse them as it shall please you, so that you do no evil to these men, because they are under the shadow of my roof" (Gen. 19:8).

Joseph Smith Translation: "I have two virgin daughters. I pray and plead with you that I may not bring them unto you and you shall not do unto them as you wish. Let me plead with you also that you do nothing to these men."

It is egregious to suggest that Lot would allow the rape of his two daughters in order to prevent the homosexual abuse of his male guests.

King James Bible: "And the Lord said thou canst not see my face, for no man shall see me and live" (Exodus 33:10).

Joseph Smith translation: "No man has seen God at any time, except those who believe. No sinful man has seen God."

Jesus said: "As it is written in the book of the words of Esaias the prophet, saying, The voice of one crying in the wilderness, Prepare ye the away of the Lord, make his paths straight . . . And begin not to say within yourselves: We have Abraham to our father" (Luke 3:4, 8).

Joseph Smith Translation: *"Prepare the way of the Lord, for He shall come as written in the book of the prophets: To take away the sins of the world; To bring salvation to heathen nations; To gather those that are lost who are of Israel and make possible the preaching to gentiles; To bring about the resurrection of the dead; To administer justice to all; To convince the ungodly of their sins. All flesh shall see the salvation of God."*

"And it came to pass when the evil spirit from God . . ." (Isaiah 16:23).

"When the evil spirit from God . . ." (1 Sam. 18:10).

"Now behold, the Lord hath put a lying spirit in the mouth of these prophets."

These were corrected by Joseph Smith: *"When the evil spirit, which was not of God . . ."*

"When the evil spirit, which was not of God . . ."

"All manner of sin and blasphemy shall be forgiven" (Matt 12:31).

Joseph Smith Translation: *"All manner of sin and blasphemy shall be forgiven unto men who receive me and repent."*

Many Catholics and Christians believe the sacrament to be the actual body and blood of Christ: *"Take eat, this is my body. Drink of this, for this is my blood"* (Matt. 26:22).

THE SACRAMENT PRAYER IN
LATTER-DAY SAINT CHURCHES

"O God, the Eternal Father, we ask thee in the name of thy Son, Jesus Christ to bless and sanctify this bread to the souls of all those who partake of it; that they may eat in remembrance of the body of thy Son and witness unto thee, O God, the Eternal Father, that they are willing to take upon them the name of thy Son, and always remember him, and keep his commandments, which He hath given them, that they may always have his Spirit to be with them (B.O.M., Moroni 4:3).

The manner of administering the wine (water):

O God, the Eternal Father, we ask thee, in the name of thy Son, Jesus Christ, to bless and sanctify this wine (water) to the souls of all those who drink of it, that they may do it in remembrance of the blood of thy Son, which was shed for them, that they may witness unto thee, O God, the Eternal Father, that they do always remember him, that they may have his Spirit to be with them. Amen (B.O.M., Moroni 5:1).

Chapter 8

ARE MORMONS CHRISTIANS?

Many non Mormons claim Mormonism is a cult. They claim it is a weird religion consisting of people who practice polygamy and believe in a different Bible.

MORMON CHRISTIANITY

1. Mormons believe Christ is the Only Begotten Son of God.
2. Mormons affirm the Godhood of Christ. He is divine.
3. Mormons believe Christ has risen, that He died for us.
4. Mormons believe Christ took upon Himself the sins of mankind.
5. Mormons pray in the name of Christ.
6. Mormons baptize in the name of Christ.
7. Mormons perform all their ordinances in the name of Christ.
8. Mormons dedicate all their churches and temples in the name of Christ.
9. Mormons believe that God and Christ are anthropomorphic. They have bodies like man, albeit immaculate and purified.
10. Mormons believe that the possible potential of men and women is godhood. "As man is God once was. As God is man may become."
11. The Book of Mormon is a witness of Christ, affirming the Bible.

The name of the Mormon Church is The Church of Jesus Christ of Latter-day Saints. Whom do they say is the head of the church? Jesus Christ.

The teachings of Jesus Christ are fundamental to the beliefs of all Mormons. Latter-day Saints believe that Christ will return to earth. They believe He will convert the Jews and Muslims as well as the rest of mankind as they receive His message and see His proof that He is the Messiah and died for mankind and atoned for the sins of the world.

Jesus will overcome the forces of evil, and Satan and his forces will be overcome. Jesus is the Son of God. He is the Creator of this earth under the direction of God the Father. He is the Savior. He is Jehovah, the God of Israel. He is our Judge and our Redeemer.

Chapter 9

KORAN, BIBLE, AND MORMONISM

The Doctrine and Covenants are revelations given to Joseph Smith, the Prophet, with some additions by his successors in the presidency of the Church.

Muslims believe the Koran to be the word of God given to Muhammad via the angel Gabriel. It was compiled from traditions and pieces of parchment by Muhammad's followers after his death. *"If they say 'He invented it by himself,' 'Say to them: Produce ten invented chapters like it. But if they fail, know that it is revealed with God's knowledge and that there is no God but Him. Will you then accept Islam?"* (K 11:9).

The Koran has been praised, worshiped, or ridiculed ever since it was compiled some years after Muhammad died. It has been quoted, misquoted, revered, called the word of God and a work of the devil.

THE KORAN EXPLAINS THE SCRIPTURES

Muslims say: *"The Koran could not have been devised by any but God. It confirms what was revealed before it and fully explains the Scriptures. It is beyond doubt from the Lord of the Universe"* (K 10:35).

"Such was Jesus son of Mary; God forbid that He Himself should beget a son! When he decrees a thing He need only say; 'Be' and it is" (K 19:34).

"The unbelievers ask: 'Why was the Koran not revealed to him entirely in a single revelation?' We have revealed it thus so that We may sustain your heart. We have imparted it to you by gradual revelation" (K 25:31).

"The Koran could not have been devised by any but God. It confirms what was revealed before it and fully explains the Scriptures. It is beyond doubt from the Lord of the Universe" (K 10:55).

THE WORD OF GOD

"Thus we have revealed it, a code in the Arabic tongue" (K 13:34).

Muslims believe the Koran to be the word of God as given to Muhammad. Jews believe the Torah to be the word of God.

Mormons believe the Bible is the word of God as long as it is translated correctly, and they accept the King James Version, although also referring to the Joseph Smith Translation—a translation of the Bible which he never completed.

Detractors have claimed that the Koran is merely a repetition of stories from the Bible, especially the Old Testament. Some, like Salman Rushdie have called it "Satanic Verses."

H.G. Wells described Muhammad as "A man of very considerable vanity, greed, cunning, self-deception and quite sincere religious passion. . . A shifty character."

John Keegan, in *A History of Warfare*, says, "Muhammad, unlike Christ, was a man of violence, he bore arms, was wounded in battle and preached holy war, Jihad, against those who defied the will of God as revealed to him."

Undoubtedly Muhammad was highly intelligent, very charismatic, loved the Arab people, and was well acquainted with the scriptures. He was a great warrior, as were many

28

medieval leaders, and was responsible for starting one of the great religions of the world. He was disgusted with the worship of multiple gods and became convinced there is only one God, thus supporting the beliefs of the other two great monotheistic religions: Judaism, which was begun at least 2500 years previously, and Christianity, which had its roots in Judaism, which began 700 years before Islam.

Muslims think of Muhammad as a humble religious man, a man of faith, a gentle man. The Muhammad of history is very different. He was a man with great charisma, a warrior, who used war and terror to achieve his power. He loved Arabs and his country, and fought against his enemies using the name of God. His followers spread Islam with a sword in one hand and the Koran in the other. Napoleon and Alexander hoped to conquer the world, but they didn't invoke religion.

Unfortunately, many Muslim fundamentalists still want to have one religion, one law, and are willing to use the tactics of violence and force, all in the name of God, like their leader, Muhammad. People of today have tasted liberty and are not willing to have their lives completely controlled by theocracies controlled by religious leaders.

Contrasted with this is the admonition of Christ, who said, *"Give unto Caesar what is Caesar's, and unto God what is God's"* (Luke 20:22).

The American Constitution, which Mormons believe was written under the direction of God, forbids having a state religion. Unlike Islamic controlled theocracies, in which officials claim divine sanction, religious freedom is sacrosanct to Americans and other democracies.

Chapter 10

WHO IS GOD?

Muslims, Jews, and Christians believe God created the heavens and the earth. Mormons believe He has created many earths besides the one we live on.

HOW CAN PEOPLE DENY THAT GOD HAS A BODY LIKE OURS?

Most religions teach that God is some kind of spirit, without body and is not anthromorphic. Despite the fact that God has appeared to prophets and groups of people throughout history, many still deny He has a human form, although He said that He created man in His own image.

"And the Lord spake to Moses face to face as a man speaketh to his friend" (Exodus 11:33).

Mormons believe God has a body, albeit resurrected, who had a mortal experience like us. They believe He is exactly as Jesus described Him: *"If you see me you see the Father"* (John 14:9).

"God The Father has a body of flesh and bones as tangible as man's; the Son also; but the Holy Ghost has not a body of flesh and bones, but is a personage of Spirit. Were it not so, the Holy Ghost could not dwell in us" (D&C 130:22).

God is not some ethereal force or mysterious nirvana or condition. He is a man omniscient. He has created many earths. He is the Father of our spirits.

MOTHER IN HEAVEN

The Koran states that Christ could not be the Begotten Son of God because God has no consort. However, the Old Testament confirms that there is a Queen of Heaven:

> *"Thus saith the Lord of hosts, the God of Israel: Ye and your wives have both spoken with your mouths, saying, We will surely perform our vows that we have vowed, to burn incense to the queen of heaven, and to pour out drink offerings unto her"* (Jer. 44:25).

Mormons also believe we have a Mother in Heaven who was a co-creator of our spirits. One of the hymns of Latter-day Saints is *O My Father*:

> *In the heavens are parents single?*
> *No, the thought makes reason stare.*
> *Truth is reason, truth eternal*
> *Tells me I've a mother there.*

Latter-day Saints (Mormons) believe intelligences are eternal and existed with God before receiving their spiritual bodies from God. *"Man was also in the beginning with God. Intelligence or the light of truth, was not created or made, neither indeed can be"* (D&C 93:29).

Matthew 5:58 in the Bible personifies the potentiality of man: *"Be ye therefore perfect, even as your Father which is in heaven is perfect."*

Jesus taught that perfection is possible. Mormons believe men and women may become gods and goddesses, although never attaining the stature or equality of God.

GOD AND THE KORAN:

"God is forgiving and merciful" (K 3:29).

"The term of every life is fixed" (K 3:140).

"It is God who ordains life and death" (K 3:156).

"There is no blessing you which does not come from God" (K 16:45).

"Know that God restores the earth to life after its death" (K 57:13).

"Every misfortune that befalls the earth, or your own person is ordained" (K 57:21).

"Every leaf that falls is known to Him" (K 6:59).

Chapter 11

POTENTIAL FOR GODHOOD

One of the most important Mormon tenets is: *"As man is, God once was. As God is man may become"* (Joseph Smith and Lorenzo Snow).

"Then shall they be gods (men and women) and have no end, because they continue" (D&C 132:20).

Deuteronomy refers to God as one of Many gods: *"For the Lord your God is God of gods, and Lord of lords"* (Deut. 10:17).

> *"O give thanks unto the God of gods: for his mercy endureth forever"* (Psalm 136:2).

> *"If you deny yourselves of all ungodliness and love God with all your might, mind and strength—you are perfect in Christ, and you can in nowise deny the power of God"* (Moroni 10:32).

> *"I have said Ye are gods; and all of you are children of the most High"* (Psalm 82:6).

Jesus quoted this Psalm and interpreted the term gods as referring to human beings who had been righteous enough and attained perfection enough that they could be called gods. *"Jesus said, is it not written in our law, I said, Ye are gods? If he called them gods, unto whom the word of God came, and the scripture cannot be broken; say ye of him, whom the Father hath sanctified, and sent into the world, Thou blasphemist; because I said I am the Son of God?"* (John 10:34, 36).

Mormons thus believe that human beings can, whether in this life or the next, attain perfection enough to attain the power and authority of God and can properly be called gods. They can never become equal to God, but may, as His children, perhaps help, under His direction and through Jesus Christ in the preparation of other earths.

SCIENCE AND SPIRITUALITY

Recent scientific studies shown that in the parietal region of the human brain changes occur during intense spiritual experiences. (See Readers' Digest. *Searching for the Divine.* December, 2001).

When God created men and women, He possibly made a small area in their brain in which God could be reached and God could influence human beings.

"The Lord is my light and my salvation" (Psalms 27:1).

"I am the light of the world" (John 8:12).

"Light is come into the world and men love darkness" (John 3:19).

"I am the true light that lighteth every man" (D&C 93:2).

"The Spirit enlighteneth every man throughout the world . . . And everyone that hearkeneth to the voice of Spirit cometh unto God, even the Father" (D&C 84:47).

Life is a roller coaster, with ups and downs, happiness and sadness, pleasure and pain. God never promised us a rose garden or that life would be without trials. In fact, He knew that the only way to grow spiritually is to overcome temptations of the flesh, adversities, and pain. He allows Satan to rule this world to see whether we can survive such a place without falling for the tricks and schemes of evil doers.

At the same time, He provided us a path to follow, with guidelines in the scriptures, and prophets through whom we could receive direction.

Chapter 12

THE ONENESS OF GOD?

Although Muslims teach oneness of God, the Koran constantly uses the plural We in referring to God:

> *"We said, 'Adam, dwell with your wife in Paradise'"* (K 2:32).

While referring to Moses, the Koran says: *We parted the sea for you. We gave Moses the scriptures. We caused the clouds to draw their shadow over you and sent down manna and quails. We delivered you from Pharaoh. We made a covenant with you. We shall test your steadfastness with fear and famine. We sent down revelations* (K 2:98) (Further references to plurality of God: KII).

> *"We shall send down the angels."*
> *"It was We that revealed the admonition."*
> *"We put doubt into the hearts of the guilty."*
> *"We have spread out the earth and set upon it immovable mountains. We have planted it."*
> *"It is surely We who ordain life and death."*
> *"We shall put terror in the hearts of the unbelievers."*

Although Jews believe in one God, the Torah, like the Koran, uses the plural in the creation of man: *"Let us make man in our own image, after our likeness"* (Gen. 1:26).

Mormons and other Christians believe Christ created the earth under the direction of God the Father:

> "And the Word was God. All things were made by him; and without him was not anything made that was made. He (Jesus) was in the world, and the world was made by him, and the world knew him not" (John 1:1,2,10).

Christ created the earth under God's direction: "For we are his workmanship, created in Christ Jesus unto good works, which God hath before ordained that we should walk in them" (Ephesians 2:10).

> "And then the Lord said: Let us go down. And they went down at the beginning, and they, that is the Gods, organized and formed the heavens and the earth.
>
> "And I, God, said unto mine Only begotten, which was with me from the beginning: Let us make man in our image, after our likeness. And I, God, created man in mine own image, in the image of mine Only Begotten created I him, male and female created I them" (Moses 2:26,27).

Chapter 13

JESUS CHRIST

Muslims and Jews do not believe in the divinity of Jesus Christ. Jews may accept him as a teacher and a Rabbi, but do not believe him to be the Messiah. Muslims accept him as a prophet, but no greater than the other prophets.

The Koran says: *"The Jews say the Christians are misguided, and the Christians say it is the Jews who are misguided, yet they both read the scriptures"* (K 2:110).

> *"We say: by no means! We believe in the faith of Abraham, and what has been revealed to Abraham, Ishmael, Isaac, Jacob, and the tribes; to Moses and Jesus and other prophets. We make no distinction among any of them. And to God we submit"* (K 2:136).

The Koran thus alludes constantly to the scriptures.

THE KORAN AND THE DIVINITY OF CHRIST

> *"They say: 'God has begotten a son. Glory be to Him! All is obedient to Him. Creator of the heavens and the earth"* (K 2:115).

> *"And now a Book confirming their own has come from God, they deny it. When they are told 'Believe in what God has revealed, they reply: 'We believe what has been revealed to us. But they deny what has since*

been revealed, although it is the truth, corroborating their own scriptures" (K 2:88).

"Admonish those that say that God has begotten a son. Surely of this they could have had no knowledge, neither they nor their fathers. A monstrous blasphemy is that which they utter. They preach nothing but false-hood" (K 18:4).

"Those that say: 'The Lord of Mercy has begotten a son preach a monstrous falsehood, at which the very heavens might crack, the earth split asunder, and the mountains crumble to dust. That they would ascribe a son to the Merciful when it does not become the Lord of Mercy to beget one!" (K 19:88).

"The angel said to Mary: 'God bids you rejoice in a Word from Him. He will instruct him in the Scriptures and in wisdom, in the Torah, and in the Gospel. He will say: 'By God's leave I will heal the blind man and the lepers, and raise the dead to life. I come to confirm the Torah, which preceded me and make lawful for you some of the things that are forbidden" (K 3:47).

THE IMMACULATE CONCEPTION

Muslims do not believe in the immaculate conception. They do not believe Christ is the Son of God.

"Lord, she said, 'How can I bear a child when no man has touched me?" The angel replied: 'Even thus: God creates whom he will' (K 3:47).

"Jesus is like Adam in the sight of God. He created him from dust and the said to him: BE, and he was" (K 3:59).

Islam teaches that Christ was a prophet, like Moses, Abraham, Isaac, Ishmael, and finally, Muhammad. *"His name is the Messiah, Jesus, son of Mary. He shall be noble in this world and the world to come"* (K 3:40).

> *"Fear God and obey me. God is my Lord and your Lord"* (K 3:51).

> *"God will say: 'Jesus, son of Mary, remember the favor I bestowed on you and on your mother; how I strengthened you with the Holy Spirit; how, by My leave you healed the blind man and the leper, and by My leave restored the dead to life? Jesus, son of Mary, did you ever say to mankind: 'Worship me and my mother as gods besides God?"* (K 5:110-114).

> *"God is the Creator of the heavens and the earth. How should he have a son when He had no Consort. There is no God but Him, the creator of all things"* (K 6:100).

> *"They make of their clerics and their monks, and of the Messiah, the son of Mary, Lords besides God, though they were ordered to serve one God only. They imitate the infidels of old. God confound them ! How perverse they are!"* (K 9:27).

> *"Praise be to God who has never begotten a son; who has no partner in his Kingdom; who needs none to defend Him from humiliation"* (K 17:111).

> *"Surely they lie when they declare: 'God has begotten children. Would He choose daughters rather than sons? Will you not take heed? Have you a positive proof? Show us your scriptures if what you say be true!"* (K 37:149).

"The Messiah, Jesus, son of Mary, was no more than God's apostle and His Word which he cast to Mary: a spirit from Him. God forbid that He should have a son! God is but one God. Do not say Three. Forbear and it shall be better for you" (K 4:171).

"The Messiah, the son of Mary, was no more than an apostle. Others passed away before him. His mother was a saintly woman. They both ate earthly food" (K 5:75).

"They say: 'God has begotten a son. God forbid! Self sufficient is He" (K 10:68).

Muslims and Jews disbelieve in the Trinity: "Unbelievers are those that say, 'God is one of three. But there is but one God"* (K 5:70).

THE PROPHETS PREDICTED JESUS CHRIST

Christ was predicted by prophets of the Old Testament:

"Hear ye now, O house of David. . . the Lord himself shall give you a sign: Behold a virgin shall conceive and bear a son. . . out of the stem of Jesse. . . and shall call his name Immanuel. . . for unto us a child is born, unto us a son is given and the government shall be upon his shoulder; and his name shall be called Wonderful, Counsellor, the Mighty God, the everlasting Father, the Prince of Peace" (Isaiah 7:13,14; 9:6).

The Immaculate Conception:

"And in the sixth month the angel Gabriel was sent

from God unto a city of Galilee, named Nazareth to a virgin espoused to a man whose name was Joseph, of the house of David; and the virgin's name was Mary. And the angel said unto her, Fear not, Mary; for thou hast found favor with God. Behold, thou shalt conceive and bring forth a son, and shall call his name JESUS. He shall be great and shall be called the Son of the Highest. . . "And he shall reign over the house of Jacob forever. Then said Mary unto the angel, How shall this be, seeing I know not a man? And the angel answered and said unto her, The Holy Ghost shall come upon thee and the power of the Highest shall overshadow thee; therefore also that holy thing which shall be born of thee shall be called the Son of God" (Luke 1:26-35).

THE KORAN DENIES THE CRUCIFIXION OF CHRIST

"They denied the truth and uttered a monstrous falsehood against Mary. They declared: 'We have put to death the Messiah, Jesus, son of Mary, the apostle of God.' They did not kill him. They did not crucify him, but they thought they did" (K 4:157).

THE RESURRECTION AND ATONEMENT

All Christians, Muslims, and Jews believe in a resurrection and a judgement after death. Christians believe Christ died for all mankind and atoned for the sins of the world to satisfy the demands of justice.

"As for the dead, God will bring them back to life" (K 6:36).

"How can you deny God? "Did He not give you life

when you were dead, and will He not cause you to die and restore you to life?" (K 2:28).

"The unbelievers say: 'This is nothing but fables of the ancients. They declare: 'There is no other life but this; nor shall we ever be raised to life again.' Lost indeed are those who deny they will ever meet God" (K 6:26, K 6:31).

"Those that deny the life to come have faithless hearts and are puffed up with pride" (K 16:16).

"God said, 'Jesus, I am come to claim you back and lift you up to Me. I shall take you away from the unbelievers" (K 3:51).

"And ye shall know that I am the Lord, when I have opened your graves, O my people, and brought you out of your graves. And shall put my spirit in you , and ye shall live" (Ezekiel 13).

In the Book of Mormon it says:

"There is a space between death and the resurrection of the body and a state of the soul in happiness or in misery until the time which is appointed of God that the dead shall come forth, and be reunited, both soul and body, and be brought to stand before God and be judged according to their works.

"Do not suppose, because it has been spoken concerning restoration that ye shall be restored from sin to happiness. Behold I say unto you, wickedness never was happiness.

"The plan of mercy could not be brought about except an atonement should be made; therefore God himself atoneth for the sins of the world, to bring about

the plan of mercy, to appease the demands of justice, that God might be a perfect, just God, and a merciful God.

"Now how could a man repent except he should sin? How could he sin if there was no law? How could there be a law save there was a punishment?

"But there is a law given, and a punishment affixed, and repentance granted; which repentance mercy claimeth.

"Mercy cometh because of the atonement; and the atonement bringeth to pass the resurrection of the dead; and the resurrection of the dead bringeth back men unto the presence of God." (B.O.M., Alma 42).

ABRAHAM

Islam, Judaism, and Christianity recognize Abraham as the one God chose to lead His people. God told Abraham that his descendants would be as numerous as the sands on the seashore.

Mormons believe the descendants of Abraham are God's chosen people, and believe members of the Mormon church are adopted into the lineage of Abraham.

Because the Jews rejected the Savior as the Messiah, the gospel was taken to the gentiles. Gentiles who accept the gospel of Jesus Christ are counted as his people and Jews and Muslims will be the last to be converted to the Gospel of Jesus Christ and accept Him as the Messiah.

The final battle between pro-Christ and anti-Christ nations will be fought in the Middle East around Jerusalem, as predicted by prophesy. Perhaps only then will peace come between Jews and Arabs, Christians and Muslims, when Jews and Muslims are converted to Christianity by the Messiah himself. Hatred and fear will give way to love and faith. *"Strip yourselves of jealousies and fears, and humble yourselves before me, and you shall see me and know that I am"* (D&C 67:19).

Chapter 14

ADAM AND EVE

Jews, Christians, and Muslims believe God created Adam and Eve.

"We created man from dry clay, and before him Satan from smokeless fire. The Lord said to the angels: 'I am creating man from dry clay from black moulded loam. When I have fashioned him, and breathed My spirit in him, kneel down and prostate yourselves before him. The angels prostrated themselves, except Satan, who said, 'I will not bow myself to a mortal whom You have created out of dry clay, of dark moulded loam.' 'Lord,' said Satan, 'Since You have seduced me, I will tempt mankind on earth. I will seduce them all except your faithful servants" (K 15:32 and 33).

"Satan will say to them: 'True was the promise which God made you. I too made you a promise, but did not keep it. Yet I had no power over you. I only called you, and you answered me. Do not now blame me, but blame yourselves. I never believed, as you did, that I was God's equal" (K 14:22).

The Koran says that Adam named all the creatures on earth after God had told him their names: "Then said God: Adam, tell them their names" (K 2:32).

The story of the Creation and the Garden of Eden is well documented in the Bible and the Koran along with the temptation by Satan. Jews and most Christians believe the fall of Adam and Eve to temptation resulted in the curse on all mankind with the result that children are born evil.

However, Mormons believe men and women will be punished for their own sins, and not for Adam's transgression.

> "We said: 'Adam, dwell with your wife in Paradise and eat of its fruits to your heart's content wherever you will. But never approach this tree or you shall both become transgressors" (K 2:32).

> "And the Lord God took the man and put him into the Garden of Eden. And the Lord God commanded the man, saying, of every tree of the garden thou mayest freely eat; But of the tree of the knowledge of good and evil, thou shalt not eat of it; for in the day that thou eatest thereof thou shalt surely die" (Gen. 2:15,16).

> "Now Satan said to the woman: Why hath God commanded you, that you should not eat of every tree of paradise? And the woman answered him, saying: of the fruit of the trees in paradise we do eat; But of the tree which is in the midst of paradise, God hath commanded us that we should not eat; and that we should not touch it, lest perhaps we die (Gen. 3:3).

> "And Satan said to the woman: "No, you shall not die the death. For God doth know that in what day whatsoever you shall eat thereof, your eyes shall be opened and you shall be as Gods, knowing good and evil" (Gen. 3:5) (One of the few times Satan ever told the truth).

Eve knew that there could be no progress for mankind

without following the plan of God, accepted by Christ that man should have freedom of choice between good and evil—the opposite chosen by Satan in which there would be no choice. This dichotomy resulted in the war in heaven. The war for freedom of choice continues to this day, and remains the battle between good and evil.

Eve understood that man and women could never be like God or be gods without the freedom to choose the path to possible perfection. When Adam and Eve ate the special forbidden fruit, not only did they gain knowledge of good and evil, but their body structure changed. The Creator started the genetic sequences to allow reproduction. The immune system began, and because of the new environment outside the Garden, man became subject to death.

Justice prevailed when Adam and Eve were cast out of the Garden of Eden and subject to death. Mercy balanced the scales of justice through the atonement of Jesus Christ, who assumed the sins of mankind and overcame death through his crucifixion and resurrection, enabling us to make choices between good and evil with the potential of perfection and have eternal life.

Although Adam and Eve no longer had intimate contact with God, He was available to them through prayer and appeared to prophets and others throughout history.

"The Lord is my Shepherd, I shall not want. Yea, though I walk through the shadow of death I shall fear no evil, for thou art with me. Thy rod and thy staff they comfort me. . . My cup runneth over. Surely goodness and mercy shall follow me all the days of my life and I shall dwell in the house of the Lord forever" (Psalm 23).

The Koranic episode of the Garden of Eden is similar to the Bible, but in the Koran, Satan tempts both Adam and Eve: *"Satan said, 'Your Lord has forbidden you to approach this tree only to prevent you from becoming angels or immortals"* (K 7:18).

The Old Testament says: *"For God doth know that in the day ye eat thereof, then our eyes shall be opened, and ye shall be as gods, knowing good and evil"* (Gen. 3:5).

Chapter 15

THE HOLY GHOST

In the Douay (Catholic) Version of the Bible the Holy Ghost is called the Advocate. The Holy Ghost is also referred to as the Counselor, the Holy Spirit, the Spirit of God.

Mormonism teaches: *"The Father has a body of flesh and bones as tangible as man's; the Son also, but the Holy Ghost has not a body of flesh and bones, but is a personage of Spirit. Were it not so, the Holy Ghost could not dwell in us"* (D&C 131:22).

Although Islam and Judaism deny the Trinity, insisting on monotheism, the Koran is incongruent: *"God will say: 'Jesus, son of Mary, remember the favor I bestowed on you and on your mother; how I strengthened you with the Holy Spirit so that you preached to men in your cradle and in the prime of manhood; how I instructed you in the Book and in wisdom, in the Torah, and in the Gospel"* (K 5:110).

> *"We gave Jesus son of Mary indisputable signs and strengthened him with the Holy Spirit"* (K 2:250).

Muslims and Jews accept Moses as a great prophet. The Lord spoke to Moses on Mount Sinai and said, *"I have filled him with the Spirit of God in wisdom, understanding, and in knowledge, and in all manner of workmanship"* (Exodus 31:3).

In the Old Testament: *"And you shall know that I am the Lord your God . . . And I shall pour out my Spirit upon all flesh*

50

and your sons and daughters shall prophesy, your old men shall dream dreams, your young men shall see visions" (Joel 2:27,28).

 "But when the Comforter comes, whom I will send unto you from the Father, even the Spirit of truth, which proceedeth from the Father, he shall testify of me" (John 15:26).

Even Jesus, perfect as He was, received the Holy Ghost in the form of a dove when he was baptized. He used the Holy Ghost in performing miracles: *"Jesus knew their thoughts and said unto them: A house divided against itself shall not stand. If I cast out devils by the Spirit of God, then the kingdom of God is come unto you"* (Matt. 2,25,28).

 "God has revealed the things he has prepared for them that love him by His Spirit. For the Spirit searches all things, yea the deep things of God. Man knows the things of God by the Spirit of God: which things we speak, not in the words which man's wisdom teaches, but which the Holy Ghost teaches" (1 Cor. 2:10,11,13,14).

The Holy Ghost is a teacher. Jesus said, *"The Comforter, which is the Holy Ghost, whom the Father will send in my name. . . Will teach you all things and bring all things to your remembrance whatsoever I have said unto you"* (John 14:26).

Because the Old Testament was complied by scribes, and the New Testament by priests, both of whom had their own religion, wisdom, and biases, many errors were made.

"By the Holy Ghost. . . You may know the truth of all things" (B.O.M., Moroni 10:5).

Jesus taught the necessity of baptism and receiving the Holy Ghost: *"Jesus said, Except a man be born of water and of the Spirit, he cannot enter into the kingdom of God"* (John 3:5).

The Holy Ghost is available to all who are righteous: *"Let virtue garnish thy thoughts unceasingly, that your confidence will wax strong in the presence of God. Then the doctrines of the priesthood will descend upon your soul like dew from heaven, and the Holy Ghost will be your constant companion; your scepter will be a scepter of righteousness"* (D&C 121:45, 46).

What is truth and what is falsehood? *"He that diligently seeketh shall find; and the Mysteries of God shall be unfolded unto them by the power of the holy Ghost as well as if as in times to come"* (B.O.M 1 Nephi 10:19).

Gifts are given by the Holy Ghost: *"No man can say that Jesus is the Lord but by the Holy Ghost. The manifestation of the Spirit is given to every man to profit withal. For to one is given by the Spirit wisdom; to another knowledge; to another by the same Spirit faith; to another the gift of healing; by the same Spirit the working of miracles; to another prophesy, to another the discerning of spirits—all by the selfsame Spirit"* (1 Cor. 3:11).

"By the Holy Ghost you may know the truth of all things" (Mor. 10:5).

THE HOLY GHOST CAN INSPIRE PEOPLE AS IT DID COLUMBUS

"I beheld a man among the Gentiles . . . Wrought upon by the Holy Ghost and he went forth upon the

many waters unto the seed of my brethren who were in the promised land" (B.O.M., 1 Nephi 12:13).

Peace will come only if the laws of Christ and the spirit of the Holy Ghost replace the Satanic forces of envy, revenge, hatred, and jealousy.

"The fruit of the Spirit is love, joy, peace, long-suffering, gentleness, goodness, faith, meekness, and temperance. If we live in the Spirit, let us also walk in the Spirit, not desirous of vain glory, provoking one another or envying one another" (Galatians 5:22,23,25).

Chapter 16

THE SCRIPTURES

The Koran teaches that the scriptures as well as the Koran should be believed: *"Believers, have faith in God and His apostle and the Book He has revealed to his apostle and in the Scriptures He formerly revealed"* (K 4:136).

> *"To Moses We gave the Scriptures, a perfect code for the righteous, with precepts about all things, a guide and a benison, (blessing) so that they might believe in meeting their Lord. And now, We have revealed this Book truly blessed. Observe it and keep from evil, so that you may find mercy and not say: 'The Scriptures were revealed only to two communities (Jews and Christians) before us; we have no knowledge of what they read'; or: 'Had the Scriptures been revealed to us we would have been better guided that they.'*
>
> *"And who is more wicked than the man who denies the revelations of God and turns away from them. Those that turn away from Our revelations shall be sternly punished for their indifference"* (K 6:157).

Muslims accept many previous scriptures: *"We have revealed the Torah, in which there is guidance and light"* (K 5:44).

THE KORAN BORROWS MANY THINGS
FROM THE BIBLE

"We have revealed Our will to you as We revealed it to Noah and the prophets who came after him; as We revealed it to Abraham, Ishmael, Isaac, Jacob, and the tribes; to Jesus, Job, Jonah, Aaron, Solomon and David to whom We gave the Psalms" (K 4:163).

Moses especially is referred to many times in the Koran. *"God spoke directly to Moses"* (K 4:163).

"To Moses We gave the scriptures. Do not say: The Scriptures were revealed only to Jews and Christians" (K 6:117).

THE KORAN VERIFIES THAT THE BIBLE CAME FIRST

"He has already revealed the Torah and the Gospel for the guidance of mankind" (K 3:4).

"And to you we have revealed the Book with the truth. It confirms the Scriptures which came before it and stands as a guardian over them."

"We sent forth Jesus son of Mary, confirming the Torah and gave him the gospel, in which there is guidance and light, corroborating what was revealed before it in the Torah: a guide and an admonition to the righteous" (K 5:44 and 5:48).

"The Torah confirms the importance of the scriptures: "He has already reveled the Torah and the Gospel for the guidance of mankind and the distinction between right and wrong" (K 3:1).

"Those that suppress any part of the Scriptures which God has revealed in order to gain some paltry end shall swallow nothing but fire in their bellies" (K 2:173).

Christ understood the necessity of continued revelation: "Ask and it shall be given to you. Seek and ye shall find it; knock and it shall be opened unto you" (Matt. 7:7).

"He that lacks wisdom, let him ask of God, who giveth to all men liberally, and upbraideth not, and it shall be given him" (James 1:5).

Mormons believe the Bible to be the word of God as long as it is translated correctly. *"Deny not the spirit of revelation or prophesy"* (D&C 11:25).

"Satan stirs up the hearts of people to contend over the points of my doctrine. They do wrestle with the scriptures because they do not understand them, because they do no seek the Spirit of the Holy Ghost to guide them in their understanding" (D&C 10:63).

"When they are told: 'Believe in what God has revealed,' they reply: 'We believe in what has been revealed to us, but they deny what has since been revealed, although it is the truth, corroborating their own scriptures. An apostle has come to them from God confirming their own Scriptures. The Jews say the Christians are misguided, and the Christians say it is the Jews who are misguided. Yet they both read the Scriptures. Who is more wicked than the man who hides a testimony he has received from God?" (K 2:88, 2:110, and 2:136).

The Book of Mormon teaches that everyone who will believe in Christ shall become part of the chosen people of God: *"If the Gentiles should hearken unto the Lamb of God, they shall be numbered among the House of Israel and they shall be a blessed people"* (1 Nephi 14:12).

Chapter 17

INCONSISTENCIES IN THE KORAN AND TORAH

The Lord said, *"Satan doth stir up the hearts of people to contention on the points of my doctrine. In these things they do err, for they wrestle with the scriptures and do not understand them—failing to seek the Spirit of the Holy Ghost to guide them for light and understanding"* (D&C 10:63).

> *"Do you then hope that they will believe you, when some of them have already heard the Word of God and knowingly perverted it, although they understood its meaning?"* (K 2:77).

The tradition requires Muslims to face Mecca when praying. However, the Koran says: *"Righteousness does not consist in whether you face East or West"* (K 2:179).

> *"It is the devils who are unbelievers. Say to the unbelievers; 'You shall be overthrown and driven into Hell!"* (K 2:102 and K 3:8).

The Koran says: *"We will put terror into the hearts of the unbeliever"* (K 3:148). *"The day will surely come when those that disbelieve will wish that they were muslims"* (K 15:1).

Contradicting these statements: *"There are among the people of the Book (Christians) some upright men"* (K 3:113).

58

In the countries where Islam is the prominent religion and Islamic law is in effect, no other religion is tolerated. Those Muslims seem to ignore this statement in the Koran: *"There shall be no compulsion in religion"* (K 2:255). But then the Koran says: *"Those that disbelieve and deny Our revelations shall become the inmates of Hell"* (K 5:82).

Muslims believe in foreordination. Jews and most Christians believe we create our own destiny to a great extent. Jews and Mormons agree with Muslims that God knows our thoughts, and that God is omniscient, omnipotent, and omnipresent.

Young Muslims who are urged by radicals to commit suicide "in the name of God," and are taught that they will be glorified and immediately go to Paradise contradicts the Koran itself: *"Don't kill yourself"* (K 4:26). *"God knows our thoughts"* (K 3:383). Then the Koran reverses itself again: *"No one dies unless God wills. The term of every life is fixed"* (K 3:140).

Every chapter or sura in the Koran except one begins with: *"In the name of Allah, the Compassionate the Merciful."*

However, we know this doesn't square with another characteristic of God pictured in the Koran: *"God is mighty and capable of revenge"* (K 3:4).

> *"The Jews say Ezra is the son of God, while the Christians say the Messiah is the son of God. God confound them!. How perverse they are!"* (K 9:27).

However, the Koran is wrong again. Nowhere does the Torah say Ezra is the son of God. *"Ezra was the son of Seraiah, the son of Azariah, the son of Hilkiah"* (Ezra 7:1).

Ezra was a scribe who interpreted the Law of Moses: *"And Ezra the priest brought the law before the congregation"* (Nehemiah 8:2).

Islam denies the Immaculate Conception. However, this is refuted in 21:88 of the Koran, which says: *"And of the woman who kept her chastity, We breathed into her of Our spirit and made her and her son: A sign to all mankind."*

"Unbelievers are those who do not judge according to God's revelations. We decreed for them a life for a life, an eye for an eye, a tooth for a tooth, a wound for a wound" (K 5:44).

On the other hand, the Koran says: *"Believers, fulfill your duties to God and bear true witness. Do not allow your hatred for other men to turn you away from justice"* (K 5:7).

"For the man or woman who is guilty of theft, cut off their hands to punish them" (K 5:35). But then the Koran repeatedly says: *"God is forgiving and merciful"* (K 3:29).

"You shall not kill—for that is forbidden by God." But then the Koran adds a disclaimer: *"Except for a just cause"* (K 6:149).

Unfortunately, Mujahidin Muslims justify their murderous ways by claiming it is a Jihad approved by God against those who don't accept the Koran as the word of God. *"God does not love the unbelievable"* (K 3:29).

"Believers, take neither Jews or Christians as your friend. They are friends with one another. Whoever shall seek their friendship will become one of their number" (K 5:51). *"The only true faith in God's sight is Islam"* (K 3:19).

"Believers, Jews, Christians, and Sabaeans—whoever believes in God and the Last Day and does what is right shall be rewarded by their Lord. They have nothing to fear or

regret" (K 2:61). But, once again, the Koran contradicts itself: *"We will put terror in the hearts of the unbelievers"* (K 3:148).

As pointed out by Hugh Nibley in his excellent treatise in the Ensign, March, 1972, there are controversies in Islam concerning God: "A well-known teaching in Islam is that 'We came out from God and to Him we will return.'

"This has led to much controversy among Muslim theologians. How can we go from and return to Him if He is everywhere? In nothing is the dual tradition of Islam more apparent than in the division of the great teachers into two main schools, one of which insists on a completely formless and incomprehensible God while the other teaches that God has a body just like man's. The former asks, 'Can God have any attributes whatsoever without completely destroying belief in an invisible unchanging Oneness? Yet a famous teacher of the other school, Abu Amir, "Would slap on his own thigh and say (commenting on Sura 68:42) 'God has a real thigh, just like this one here.'"

The passage or Sura referred to in the Koran suggests God indeed has a body: *"Most surely, it is the Word brought by an honored Apostle (Muhammad). And if he had fabricated against Us (God), We would have certainly seized him by the right hand, then we would certainly have cut off his aorta"* (K 69:45).

Christ the Messiah is the Son of God! Jesus declared it to be so 600 years before Muhammad and Islam were born, and was reaffirmed to Joseph Smith in 1820, when both the Father and the Son appeared to him.

Chapter 18

WAR AND TERROR

Radical Muslims have been engaged in a Jihad, a holy war, in which they believe God is on their side, since the beginning of Islam under Muhammad in the seventh century. We are now engaged in a continuing conflict with these extremists who have hijacked Islam and are attempting to impose their laws on the rest of the world and take away from nations who have fought many wars to obtain and preserve the freedom they enjoy.

Most Muslims are peace-loving progressive people, and often the most vociferous condemning the degenerate acts of the mujahidin.

THE KORAN PLEADS FOR PEACE

"Thou shalt not kill—for that is forbidden by God— except for a just cause" (K 6:49).

"Those that repent and mend their ways, who hold fast to God and are sincere in their devotion to God, shall be numbered among the faithful" (K 4:146).

"Do not let your hatred for other men turn you away from justice" (K 3:7).

"We decreed for them a life for a life, an eye for an eye, a nose for a nose, an ear for an ear a tooth for a tooth, a wound for a wound. But if a man charitably forbears from retaliation, his remission shall atone for him" (K 5:44).

"That is why we laid it down to the Israelites that whoever killed a human being, except as punishment for murder or other villainy shall be regarded as having killed all mankind; and that whoever saved a human life shall be regarded as having saved all mankind" (K 5:31).

"Show forgiveness, speak for justice, and avoid the ignorant. If Satan tempts you, seek refuge in God; He hears all and knows all" (K 7:199).

RADICAL ISLAMS USE THE KORAN TO JUSTIFY HOLY WAR

"God revealed His will to the angels, saying: 'I shall be with you. Give courage to the believers. I shall cast terror into the hearts of the infidels. Strike off their heads, strike off the very tips of their fingers. He that defies God and His apostle shall be sternly punished by God" (K 8:12)

"Retaliation is decreed you in bloodshed: a free man for a free man; a slave for a slave; a female for a female" (K 2:178).

"Fighting is obligatory for you, much as you dislike it, but to fight during Ramadan is a grave offense" (K 2:16).

"Prophet, make war on the unbelievers and the hypocrites and deal rigorously with them. Hell shall be their home: an evil fate" (K 9:73).

"And all those nations! We destroyed them for the wrongs they did, and for their destruction, we set a predestined time" (K 18:36).

"God will send to your aid five thousand angels splendidly accoutred, if they suddenly attack you" (K 3:125).

"Seek out the enemy relentlessly. You hope to receive from God what they cannot hope for" (K 4:103).

"We will put terror into the hearts of the unbelievers. The Fire shall be in their homes" (K 3:148).

Westerners are unable to understand Muslim terrorists who willingly commit suicide to kill others. Suicide bombers are taught if they die in a Jihad, they will go straight to Paradise. They learn ancient scripture from the Koran: *"If you do not go to war, God will punish you sternly, and will replace you by other men. Whether unarmed or well-equipped, march on and fight for the cause of God"* (K 9:37 and 9:40).

"Prophet, make war on the unbelievers" (K 9:63).

"Make war on them. God will chastise them at your hands and humble them" (K 9:12).

When the Koran says: *"Make war on them,"* (9:12), it was in reference to those who conspired to banish Muhammad from Mecca and caused him to flea with his followers to Medina. The order to make war has nothing to do with modern times, but is used by Muslim radicals, who use old medieval times and sayings to justify their Jihad of today.

"Like Pharaoh's people and those before them, they disbelieved their Lord's revelations. Therefore We will destroy them for their sins even as We drowned Pharaoh's people" (K 8:51).

Muslims believe the lands they formerly occupied rightly are theirs.

> *"Those that have embraced the Faith and fled their homes and fought for the cause of God, and those that have sheltered them and helped them—they are the true believers"* (K 8:73).

> *"Prophet, God is your strength, and the faithful who follow you. Rouse the faithful to arms. If there are twenty steadfast men with you they will vanquish two hundred. If there are a hundred they shall rout a thousand, for they are devoid of understanding. . . And if there are a thousand, they shall, by God's will, defeat two thousand. God is with those that are steadfast"* (K 8:65,66).

> *"Fight for the sake of God those that fight against you, but do not attack them first. God does not love aggressors. Slay them wherever you find them. Drive them out of the places from which they drove you"* (K 2:189).

THE JIHAD BRINGS WEALTH AS WELL AS SOULS

Paul Fregosi in his great book, *Jihad*, says, "The Jihad has been a fraud of staggering proportions, except perhaps in its early days . . . For Christians it meant either apostasy to Islam or death. The Muslims needed money more than they needed converts. It fought for the Treasury as much as for Allah. The Jihad was largely a fraud. Throughout the centuries it was one of the great triumphs of hypocrisy" (p. 109).

Those Christians and Jews who lived among the Islams in lands dominated by Muslims, were forced to pay an extra tax. Hence, some Muslims allow people of other faith to live in their land because of increased revenue, but in many Muslim countries other faiths are taboo.

THE TORAH AND WAR

War was common among the Israelites in Moses' day and God was thought to be a God of war: *"I will render vengeance to mine enemies and will regard them that hate me. I will make mine arrows drunk with blood, and my sword shall devour flesh"* (Deut. 32:41).

> *"And the Lord spake unto Moses, saying, Avenge the children of Israel. And they warred against the Midianites, as the Lord commanded Moses and they slew all the males. And the children of Israel took all the women of Midian captive and their little ones. And they burnt all their cities and took all the spoil.*
>
> *"And Moses said unto them, Have ye saved all the women alive? Now kill every male among the little ones, and kill every woman that hath known a man by lying with him. But of all the women children that have not known a man by lying with him, keep alive for yourselves"* (Numbers 31).
>
> *"But of the cities which the Lord thy God doth give thee for an inheritance, thou shalt save nothing that breatheth"* (Deut. 20:16).

Unlike radical Muslims, who use ancient suras from the Koran and Muslim traditions to justify their massacre of Jews and Christians in some countries today, Jews do not use ancient Torah scriptures to wage wars of butchery in order to survive or retake lands they anciently held.

JEWS AND PALESTINIANS HAVE IGNORED
THEIR SCRIPTURES

Although the Torah and Koran teach *"an eye for an eye,"* Jews should also remember the admonition in Leviticus: *"Thou shalt not hate thy brother in thy heart . . . Thou shalt not avenge, nor bear any grudge against the children of thy people, but thou shalt love thy neighbor as thyself. I am the Lord"* (Leviticus 19:17,18).

Muslims should remember: *"Paradise is reserved for those who pay alms in prosperity and in adversity, and for those who curb their anger and forgive their fellow men. God loves the charitable"* (K 3:132).

Those that follow the admonition of Christ replace hate with love:

"Jesus said: Ye have heard that it hath been said, Thou shalt love thy neighbor and hate thine enemy. But I say unto you, love your enemies, bless them that curse you, do good to them that hate you, and pray for them which despitefully use you and persecute you" (Matt. 5:43,44).

Jesus Christ, who appeared to people of the American continent soon after his crucifixion and resurrection said to those ancient Americans: "Think not that I am come to destroy the law or the prophets . . . It is also written before you, that thou shalt not kill, and whosoever shall kill shall be in danger of the judgment of God; But I say unto you that whosoever is angry with his brother shall be in danger of His judgment. Therefore, I would that ye should be perfect even as I, or your *"Father who is in heaven is perfect"* (3 Nephi 12).

WAR MAY BE NECESSARY TO FIGHT EVIL

Christ taught love, compassion, and forgiveness, but when attacked, the Lord justifies defending oneself and his loved ones:

"The Lord hath said: Ye shall defend your families even unto bloodshed" (Alma 44:47).

Chapter 19

HOMOSEXUALITY AND IMMORALITY

Islam, Judaism, and Christianity all condemn homosexuality:

> "If two men among you commit a lewd act, punish them both. If they repent and mend their ways, let them be. God is forgiving and merciful.
>
> "If women commit a lewd act, confine them to their houses until death overtakes them or God finds another way for them" (K 4:13 and 4:16).

> "And Lot, who said to his people: 'Will you persist in these Lewd Acts which no other nation has committed before you? You lust after men instead of women. Truly, you are a degenerate people" (K 7:76).

> "Will you Fornicate with males and eschew the wives whom God has created for you? Surely you are great transgressors" (K 26:166).

> "If a man lie with mankind, as he lieth with a woman, both of them have committed an abomination; they shall be put to death" (Leviticus 20:13).

> "In the kingdom of God there shall be no Sodomites" (Deut. 23:17).

> "Professing themselves to be wise, they became fools . . . Through the lusts of their own hearts, to

dishonor their own bodies between themselves . . . For even the women did change the natural use unto that which is against nature: and likewise also the men, leaving the natural use of woman, burned in their lust one toward another without natural affection . . . Who, knowing the judgment of God, they are worthy of death" (Romans 1:27,31,32).

"The show of their countenance doth witness against them, and doth declare their sin to be even as Sodom, and they cannot hide it. Wo unto their souls, for they have rewarded evil unto themselves" (2 Nephi 13:9).

Many homosexuals have gained political office, success in Hollywood, the arts, fashion industries, and throughout industry. Homosexuality is promoted even by educators as an alternative lifestyle. Homosexual clubs are allowed on campuses of universities, while religious clubs are not. However, no matter how much publicity and propaganda are promoted by the media and gay activists, God's laws are God's laws, and whether a Muslim, a Jew, or a Christian, it is blasphemy not to uphold and defend the immutable laws of God.

Homosexuality denies life, the family unit, and God's creation of the difference between men and women. Homophobia has become a catch word, a hate word. All murders are the result of hate, but crime against homosexuals has been given a special category known as hate crime, with greater punishment. This is "politically correct" nonsense.

Politicians have been successful in equating gay rights to civil rights. Psychiatrists claim homosexuality is a normal behavior, even possibly a genetic problem, but this has never been proven. Although many gay rightists vigorously deny it, many homosexuals have conquered their habit, just as alcoholics and drug users have overcome their behavior.

Homosexuals claim it is their "nature." Just as adultery and sexual perversion can be overcome, so, too, can homosexuality.

> Homosexuality must be genetic.
> Loudly claim the frenetic.
> They say to call it obscene
> Is discriminatory and mean.
> But, don't deny God, say Bible and Torah.
> Remember the Flood, Sodom, and Gomorrah.
> —Anonymous

> "Man-like it is to fall into sin;
> Animal-like it is to dwell therein;
> Christ-like it is for sin to grieve;
> God-like it is all sin to leave."
> —Longfellow

AIDS AND IMMORALITY

AIDS, which began in the 1980s among homosexual males, continues to ravish the world, spreading now in Asia, India, and Russia.

In Africa whole countries are being wiped out by the disease, and many of their leaders blame poverty rather than immorality.

AIDS victims, the media, governments, and activists all blame something other than the cause itself. AIDS is not due to poverty, selfish pharmaceutical companies, or racist conspiracy. Infection from blood transfusions is very rare in Western countries, and infection from dirty needles used by drug addicts occurs because the needles have been contaminated by someone with AIDS.

AIDS is the result of immoral behavior. Men get it from fellow sodomists or sexual promiscuity. Women get it from their partners. It's time we stopped making heroes out of people with AIDS.

We spend more on AIDS research than on heart disease, cancer, and arthritis combined. The cause of AIDS is sexual immorality. Certainly, we need to spend money on finding a cure or vaccine for AIDS, but especially the world needs to be educated as to the cause of AIDS and return to living God's moral laws.

ABORTION

Islamic tenet is against abortion: *"Do not slay your children for fear of poverty; We give them sustenance and yourselves; surely to kill them is a great wrong"* (K 17:31).

> *"Open thy bosom to the truth that comes. Know as soon as in the embryo, to the brain, articulation is complete. Then turn to the Prime Mover with a smile of joy on such a great work of nature. And in breathes a new spirit replete with virtue; that what here active it finds, to its own substance draws and forms an individual soul that lives—and feels—and bends, reflective on itself"* (Dante's Divine Comedy, 13th century).

Since *Roe versus Wade* there have been over 1,500,000 abortions in the United States each year, resulting in more human deaths than in all wars put together. Muslims and most Christians consider abortion an evil practice. Infanticide in late term abortion equates exactly with the ancient Muslim practice of burying unwanted female infants alive.

Mormons believe abortion is an unholy and sinful act except in cases where the life of the mother is at stake, or in cases of rape or incest.

Catholic Archbishop O'Conner in a talk several years ago said: "The Founding Fathers acted under the influence of a benevolent Creator, basing the Declaration of Independence and the Constitution on natural moral laws, which would pre-empt all laws enacted by politicians or governmental bodies, or privately interpreted by Supreme Court Justices."

Mormons believe America was founded under the direction of God.

> *"The United States Constitution was written by men who accepted Jesus Christ as the Savior of mankind. Americans have an obligation to preserve not only the Constitution, but also the Christian principles from which sprang that immortal document."* (David O. McKay, former President of the Church of Jesus Christ of Latter-day Saints).

"Thou shalt not kill." The Ten Commandments plus the teachings of Christ apply to abortion. God's laws do not change to fit changing times.

Chapter 20

WOMEN

Islam is perhaps the most repressive system against women the world has ever seen. In ancient times Muslim girl babies were buried alive. Women in many Islamic theocracies are forbidden to go to school, forbidden to work, and are required to cover their faces and bodies when in public.

"Women are your Fields; go, then, into your fields whence you please" (K 2:222).

"Men have authority over women because God has made one superior over the other. Good women are obedient. They cover their unseen parts because God has guarded them. As for those from whom you fear disobedience, forsake them in beds apart and beat them" (K 4:34).

At the same time the Koran teaches Muslims to honor women: *"Those that defame honorable but careless women shall be cursed in this world and in the world to come. Good women are for good men, and good men for good women"* (K 24:23 and 24).

"Prophet enjoin your wives, your daughters and the wives of true believers to draw their veils close around them" (K 33:57).

"Enjoin believing women to turn their eyes away

from temptation and to preserve their chastity; not to display their adornments; to draw their veils over their bosoms except to their husbands—and children who have no carnal knowledge of women. And let them not stamp their feet when walking so as to reveal their hidden trinkets" (K 24:3).

This is similar to Isaiah 3:6,18: *"Moreover the Lord saith, Because the daughters of Zion are haughty, and walk with stretched forth necks and wanton eyes, walking and mincing as they go, and making a tinkling with their feet."*

In Judaism only men study the Torah. However, women in modern Israel have played prominent roles in all society. They are part of the military and receive higher secular education.

WOMEN AND CHRISTIANITY

"In the last days, saith God, I will pour out my spirit upon all flesh; and your sons and daughters shall prophesy" (Acts 2:17).

No woman is revered as much as Mary, the mother of Jesus. Other prominent women during the Savior's reign included Elizabeth, Mary's cousin, Mary Magdalene, and Martha.

"Now there stood by the cross of Jesus his mother, and his mother's sister, Mary, the wife of Cleophas, and Mary Magdalene" (John 19:25).

On the other hand, in First Corinthians, we learn of the inferior role of women: *"For God is not the author of confusion, but of peace, as in all the churches of the saints. Let your women keep silence in the churches, for it is not permitted unto them to speak; but they are commanded to be under obedience, as also saith the law. And if they will learn any thing, let them ask their husbands at home; for it is a shame for women to speak in the church"* (1 Cor. 14:33,34,35).

However, also in Corinthians: *"Neither the man was created for the woman; but the woman for the man. For this cause ought the woman to have power on her head because of the angels"* (1 Cor. 11:9).

"Husbands, love your wives and be not bitter against them" (Col. 3:19).

Fortunately, some moderate Muslim countries are abandoning this cruel discrimination and providing a more egalitarian society.

In the LDS church, women participate equally in giving prayers, sermons, leading the music, singing in choirs, greeting visitors, and teaching classes. They do not administer the Sacrament or perform ordinances reserved for men holding the priesthood.

Although the LDS church has opposed the Equal Rights Amendment (ERA), agreeing with most state legislatures that it would cause havoc by overloading the judicial system, the church has always advocated equal pay for equal work, and non-discrimination against women. Utah gave voting rights to women long before many other states or territories.

The Relief Society of the church, devoted to compassionate service fore the sick, poor, or homeless, and committed to continuous education for women, was organized in 1848, the first of its kind in the nation.

Education for Mormon women has always been of great importance. "We believe women are useful, not only to do housework and raise babies, but they should study law or physics, be able to do business in any counting house, and all this to enlarge their sphere of usefulness for the benefit of society at large. In following these things they but answer the design of their creation" (Brigham Young sermon 18 July 1869, in *Journal of Discourses*, 13:61).

Chapter 21

HEAVEN AND HELL

Muslims, Jews, and Christians believe in life after death. The Koran teaches that there are seven heavens. *"Then He directed Himself to the heaven and it is a vapor, so He said to it and the earth, Come both willingly or unwillingly. They both said We come willingly. So He ordained them seven heavens in two periods, and revealed in every heaven its affair; and We adorned the lower heaven with brilliant stars and (made it) to guard; That is the decree of the Mighty, the Knowing"* (K 41:11,12).

> *"Are you content with this life in preference to the life to come? Few indeed are the blessings of this life compared to the life to come.*
> *"If you do not go to war, He will punish you sternly and will replace you with other men"* (K 9:37).

> *"God has promised the men and women who believe in Him gardens watered by running streams, in which they will abide forever; goodly mansions in the Garden of Eden, and what is more they will have grace in God's sight. That is the supreme triumph"* (K 9:72).

The Koran speaks mainly about men who reach paradise. They will be adorned in beautiful clothes and jewels, and will lounge on silk laden couches with nubile well endowed virgins.

They will drink beverages which will not cause drunkenness, served by young handsome boys. Their love making with the virgins will go on forever.

Women in heaven other than the young virgins are not mentioned except they will be with the righteous living in mansions next to running streams of water. There are no old and no children in heaven. Those who make it are forever young and handsome and virile.

Islam Fundamentalists promise those who die in a Jihad will go straight to Paradise and lounge on silken couches with beautiful girls:

> "The true servants of God shall be well provided for, feasting on fruit, and honored in the gardens of delight. Reclining face to face upon soft couches, they shall be served with a goblet filled at a gushing fountain, white and delicious. It will neither dull their senses nor befuddle them. They shall sit with bashful, dark eyed virgins. They will put questions to each other. One will say: 'I had a friend who used to ask:' Do you really believe? And he will say: 'Come let us look down.' He will look down and see his friend in the very midst of hell" (K 17:47,48).

This view of paradise is repeated several times in the Koran:

> "The righteous shall return to a blessed retreat: the gardens of Eden, whose gates shall be open wide to receive them. Reclining there with bashful virgins for companions, they will call for abundant fruit and drink" (K 38:44).

> "As for the righteous, they shall be lodged in peace

together amid gardens and fountains, arrayed in rich silks and fine brocade. Even thus: and We shall wed them to dark eyed Houris. Secure against all ills, they shall call for every kind of fruit and having died once, they shall die no more" (K 44:43).

"You shall enter gardens watered by running streams in which you shall abide forever." (K 57:7).

"And there shall wait upon them young boys of their own, as fair as virgin pearls" (K 52:13).

"The life of this world is but a sport and a diversion" (K 47:34).

The Koran teaches that unbelievers will go to hell where they will be constantly burned by fire and drink boiling water. *"But doleful shall be the return of the transgressors. They shall burn in hell. There let them taste their drink: scalding water, festering blood, and other putrid things"* (K 38:44).

"Those that wrong the Apostle of God will be sternly punished. And shall abide forever in the fire of Hell" (K 9:63)

"We have adorned the lowest heaven with lamps, missiles to pelt the devils with. We have prepared the scourge of fire for these and for those who deny their Lord" (K 67:4).

"Your God is one God. Those that deny the life to come have faithless hearts and are puffed up with pride" (K 16:16).

"Burn him in the Fire of Hell, then fasten him with a chain seventy cubits long. For he did not believe in God nor feed the destitute. Today he shall be friendless

here; only filth shall be his food" (K 69:19).

"Your hearts are taken up with worldly gain from cradle to grave" (K 102:1).

APOSTASY FROM ISLAM IS DANGEROUS

"Those who deny God after professing Islam and open their bosoms to unbelief shall incur the wrath of God; grievous punishment awaits them" (K 16:102).

"Have you heard of the Event (Last Days) which will overwhelm mankind? On that day there shall be downcast faces, of men broken and worn out, burnt by a scorching fire, drinking from a seething fountain. Their only food shall be bitter thorns, which will neither sustain them nor satisfy their hunger.

"On that day there shall be radiant faces, of men well-pleased with their labors, in a lofty garden. There they shall hear no idle talk. A gushing fountain shall be there, and raised soft couches with goblets placed before them; silken cushions ranged in order and carpets richly spread" (K 87:19 and 88:1).

JEWS AND CHRISTIANS AND HEAVEN

"In the beginning God made the heaven and the earth" (Gen. 1:1).

"And God called the firmament heaven" (Gen. 1:8).

"Behold, the heaven of the heavens is the Lord's. The earth also" (Deut. 10:14).

"How art thou fallen from heaven, O Lucifer?" (Isaiah 14:12).

The Lord said to Job: *"Knowest thou the ordinances of heaven? Canst thou set the dominion thereof in the earth?"* (Job 38:33).

"Yea, though I walk through the shadow of death, I shall fear no evil. Thy rod and thy staff they comfort me. Surely goodness and mercy shall follow me all the days of my life and I shall dwell in the house of the Lord forever" (Psalm 23:4,6).

Jesus said to them:

"Verily, verily, I say unto you, He that heareth my word and believeth on him that sent me, hath everlasting life, and shall not come into condemnation; but is passed from death unto life. Verily, verily, I say unto you, The hour is coming and now is when the dead shall hear the voice of the Son of God; and they that hear shall live. For as the Father hath life in himself; so hath He given to the Son to have life in himself; Marvel not at this: for the hour is coming, in the which all that are in the graves shall hear his voice, and shall come forth; they that have done good, unto the resurrection of life; and they that have done evil, unto the resurrection of the damnation.

"Search the scriptures, for in them ye think ye have eternal life.

"Do not think that I will accuse you to the Father. There is one that accuseth you, even Moses, in whom ye trust. For had ye believed Moses, ye would have believed me. For he wrote of me. But if ye believe not his writings, how shall ye believe my words?" (John 5).

MORMONISM AND THE KINGDOMS OF HEAVEN

Mormons believe that an all-caring, all-loving, all-merciful God provides not only life eternal to all men, women, and children by the crucifixion and resurrection, and by the atonement of Jesus Christ, but also the possibility for all of his children to achieve celestialization, which is eternal life living with God. The three kingdoms of heaven or degrees of glory, depending on our behavior on earth are the Telestial, Terrestrial, and the Celestial.

TELESTIAL

Inhabiting the Telestial nation will be vast numbers of people: "Innumerable as the stars in the heaven or as the sand upon the seashore." These are they who do not deny the Holy Spirit, but fail to receive the gospel of Christ. Some worshipped ancient gods such as Apollo or Cepheus, some remain agnostic or atheistic, believing in humanism and nature, rather than in a Creator.

Others hear the message of Christ, but fail to obtain or retain a testimony of Jesus, falling prey to the cacophony of false teachers and the "intelligentsia." They treat the gospel messages as though they were from the Delphic oracle.

Also numbered among those in the Telestial society are the greedy, the blasphemers, unrepentant adulterers, sexual perverts, and those who fail to listen to the prophets. They believe in the laws of man rather than the laws of God.

Counted among the Telestialites are those that wait in hell until the Savior has perfected his work in the fullness of times, at which time their permanent dwelling place will be prepared when they are judged. They will be servants of God, but unable to live in or visit the higher kingdoms of heaven.

TERRESTRIAL

The Terrestrial abode after resurrection will be the home of honorable men and women who are nevertheless blinded by misguided philosophers or teachers, who, though believing in Jesus Christ, lack sufficient testimony of him. They are good people who have an insouciant attitude toward the advice of the prophets. Also, their presence in the Terrestrial may be temporary, depending on their conversion and good works. These are the spirits of men and women in "prison" whom the Messiah visited and taught His gospel, that they may be judged as though they were still mortal.

CELESTIAL

The Celestial kingdom will be the home of worthy men and women, made perfect through Jesus, by keeping the covenants made with Him, baptized by immersion in His name, keeping all the commandments of God, overcoming sin by faith and repentance, and sealed by the Holy Spirit in temples of the Lord built for that purpose, and are known as members of the Church of the Firstborn. They shall have part in the first resurrection and dwell forever in the awesome presence of God and Jesus Christ. By continuing the perfection processes they began while on earth, they may eventually obtain godhood and perhaps be servants of God or Christ in the creation of other worlds.

Mormons believe in baptism by proxy for the dead as well as proxy doing other ordinances necessary for celestialization. These are done in their temples for those in Paradise. Those who accept the gospel of Jesus Christ, may, depending on their repentance and worthiness, achieve the Celestial Kingdom.

God sent the following messengers to give us the keys to the Celestial Kingdom:

1. The angel Moroni, to show Joseph Smith where the Book of Mormon was hidden in the hill near his home. This book contains an additional witness to the Bible of the divinity of Jesus Christ and the fullness of His gospel.

2. Elias, who restored those things spoken of by the holy prophets to prepare for the last days.

3. John the Baptist to restore the Aaronic Priesthood.

4. Elijah, to emphasize the importance of genealogy and to begin performing by proxy in holy temples those ordinances necessary for the exaltation of our kindred dead and their possible celestialization.

5. Joseph, Jacob, Isaac, and Abraham, to fulfill the Lord's promises. Those who are baptized by authority and receive the Holy Ghost become adopted into the family of Abraham, becoming part of God's chosen people.

6. Adam, with special keys to the kingdom of God and Jesus Christ.

7. Peter, James, and John, members of Christ's first presidency when He was on earth, to restore the Melchizedek Priesthood—the priesthood and power of Jesus Christ, to act for and in behalf of God the Father.

"During the early days of the church we passed through a period of slander and we came through. We passed through a period of mobs and bloodshed and we survived. We passed through poverty, and gained strength. Then we passed through the age of apostasy and betrayed from the inside, one of the severest tests. We are now going through another trial—a period which we might call sophistication. This is a time when many clever people will not listen to the words of the prophet." (Harold B. Lee, former President of the Church. June, 1965).

Hell is reserved for the Sons of Perdition, those who have received the Holy Ghost and then deny it. They do not receive a resurrected body.

Chapter 22

POLYGAMY AND ADULTERY

The custom of having plural wives was common among the prophets of the Old Testament, and is common among Muslims today. While polygamy is acceptable among believers in Islam, adultery is punishable by death. Adultery in the Mormon church is cause for excommunication.

While the Ten Commandments said, *"Thou shalt not commit adultery,"* Christ said that to look at a woman with lust is committing adultery in a man's heart. When Jesus came upon the mob who was about to stone a woman to death, He said, *"Let him who is without sin cast the first stone."* The mob turned away in shame and Jesus turned to the woman and said, *"Go thy way and sin no more."*

The Koran advocates polygamy:

"Try as you may, you cannot treat all your wives impartially" (K 4:26).

"You may marry other women who seem good to you: two, three, or four of them. But if you fear you cannot maintain equality among them, marry only one or any slave girls you may own" (K 4:1).

"You may put off any of your wives you please and take to your bed any of them you please" (K 35:51).

"You must not speak ill of God's apostle, nor shall you ever wed his wives after him" (K 35:53).

In today's Western culture we see adultery and promiscuity, premarital sex, and homosexuality accepted as almost normal behavior on television, in movies, and on the printed page. Women have become sex objects, and nudity and pornography are rampant on the television screen. Unfortunately, the portrayal of American life is too often judged by our movies and some of the trashy music we export. The freedoms guaranteed by our Constitution are too often abused by musicians, authors, movie and television producers, and artists, who give America a bad name. Muslims are somewhat justified in claiming that America is a degenerate, satanistic country, breaking God's laws and worshiping materialism.

The practice of polygamy among Mormons began in the 1840s, following a revelation to Joseph Smith to restore the Biblical custom of ancient prophets. Joseph Smith agonized over this for several years before instituting polygamy until an angel appeared to him, warning him that he must do so.

Being of Puritanical background, many Mormons greeted this new precept with skepticism and reluctance, and many left the church. Joseph's own brother, Hyrum Smith, said, "It's the work of the devil," but he finally accepted it. Brigham Young was at first one of polygamy's staunchest foes, but finally accepted it as a commandment from God. He said, "It was the first time in my life I wished for the grave."

The word "Mormon" became, and still is, associated with polygamy, although it was practiced only for a few years, being discontinued by church President Wilford Woodruff in 1890, on instructions from the Lord.

While polygamy was at one time acceptable Mormon church doctrine, premarital sex, adultery, homosexuality, and immoral behavior have always been considered grievous sins and the basis for excommunication.

Early members of the church were treated with scorn,

hatred, and persecution. They were beaten, killed, and driven from their homes, causing them to move from New York to Illinois, Ohio, Missouri, and finally to the barren desert country of Utah Territory. They lost their homes, property, and their lives. The state of Missouri only recently rescinded an old law calling for the extermination of all Mormons.

The Bill of Rights of the Constitution—guaranteeing the right to practice religion according to the dictates of one's own conscience—was made a mockery at the time Mormons practiced polygamy. The Supreme Court decision, *Reynolds versus the United States* maintained that society has the right to forbid the practice of polygamy, even though it might be a part of religious belief.

Why was polygamy acceptable by God among the prophets and people of ancient Israel and during the early period of the Mormon church? While this cannot be fully answered, perhaps some answers can be surmised.

At the time of Abraham and later prophets, it was necessary for God's chosen people to increase in number and strength. Women probably outnumbered men because of wars. Adultery was forbidden, but taking more than one wife and wives of lesser stature (concubines) was allowed.

At the beginning of the Mormon church there was an urgent need for rapid church membership. Unmarried women or widows, who might be denied marriage and security were given the opportunity to be part of a family unit.

Polygamy made the Mormons a tried people. Polygamous families, by necessity, became God-fearing, industrious, unselfish, and community minded. Polygamy was a practice among only 5 percent of the members of the church, and only by those men who were worthy and financially able to support an additional wife.

POLYGAMY IS NO LONGER ACCEPTABLE

"Behold, David and Solomon had many wives and concubines, which was abominable to me. Wherefore, I the Lord God will not suffer the people to be like unto them of old. Wherefore, by brethren, hear me and hearken unto the word of the Lord—For there shall not any man among you have save it be one wife, and concubines he shall have none. I the Lord delight in the chastity of women and whoredoms are an abomination before me" (B.O.M., Jacob 2:24,28).

As stated previously, the Lord instructed Joseph Smith to institute polygamy among worthy men to build up the church and provide homes for women, including widows. Concubines, adultery, and prostitution were always forbidden. After the Mormons came to Utah and the church was well established, God instructed through His prophet to stop polygamy and make polygamy cause for excommunication for those who disobeyed Him.

"For they have not forgotten the commandment of the Lord, which was given unto our father—that they should have save it were one wife and concubines they should have none; and there should not be whoredoms committed among them" (B.O.M., Jacob 3:5).

"Wherefore my brethren, hear me and hearken to the word of the Lord: For there shall not any man among you have save it be one wife; and concubines he shall have none" (Jacob 2:27).

"Abraham had concubines who bore him children... Because they were given to him, and he

abode in my law, as Isaac and Jacob. . . David also received many wives and concubines, and also Solomon and Moses., as also many other of my servants from the creation . . . And in nothing did they sin save in those things they received not of me" (D&C 132:37,38).

"Whoso forbiddeth to marry is not ordained of God, for marriage is ordained of God for man. Wherefore, it is lawful that he have one wife, and they twain shall be one flesh, and all this that the earth might answer the end of its creation" (D&C 49:15,16).

Polygamy by Mormons today results in excommunication. Polygamy in the beginning of the church was a test of obedience. Its discontinuance was again a test of obedience. No member of the Mormon church today is a polygamist.

MORMONISM ON ABORTION AND WELFARE

The LDS Church has a huge and successful welfare system, an adoption agency, and an active program to help the homeless find homes and jobs. Millions of tons of food and clothing are sent annually to needy people all over the world. Its charity programs have helped people everywhere.

Mormonism does not allow abortion except in cases of a threat to the mother's life, or in cases of rape or incest. Utah has the lowest venereal disease rate in the country as well as the lowest abortion rate, and the lowest number of children who are removed from a home because of abuse.

Chapter 23

FOOD AND FANTASIES

Muslims and Jews have strict food laws. They are not allowed to eat pork, products of the sea which do not have fins, camels or animals which don't chew the cud or have split hooves.

> *"It is lawful to eat all wholesome foods and food which is in the Book"* (K 3, 5:5).
>
> *"Believers, eat of the wholesome things with which We have provided you and give thanks to God, if it is Him you worship. He has forbidden you carrion, blood and the flesh of swine"* (K 2:168).
>
> *"Eat and drink but avoid excess. God does not love the intemperate"* (K 7:20).
>
> *"Wine and games of chance are abominations devised by Satan"* (K 5:90).

The Torah, like the Koran, advises against use of alcohol: *"Do not drink wine or strong drink"* (Lev. 10:9).

MUSLIM AND JEWISH FOOD LAWS

Jewish dietary law is spelled out in Leviticus. In addition, food shall be prepared according to rabbinic law, ritually pure, and Kosher. Kosher is from the Hebrew word kasher, meaning proper.

"These are the beasts which ye shall eat among all the beasts that are on the earth: Whatsoever parteth the hoof and is cloven footed, and cheweth the cud, among the beasts that shall ye eat. Nevertheless these shall ye not eat of them that chew the cud, or of them that divide the hoof: as the camel, because he cheweth the cud, but divideth not the hoof; he is unclean unto you. And the coney, and the hare, and the swine.

"These shall ye eat of all that are in the waters; whatsoever hath fins and scales in the waters, in the seas and in the rivers, them shall ye eat. Whatsoever hath no fins or scales in the waters, that shall be an abomination unto you.

"And these are they which ye shall have an abomination among the fowls. They shall not be eaten, they are an abomination: The eagle, the ossifarage, the osprey, the vulture, the kite, every raven after his kind, and the owl, and the night hawk, and the cuckoo, and the hawk after his kind. And the little owl, and the cormorant, and the great owl, and the swan, and the pelican, and the stork, also fowls that creep, going on all four.

"Even these of them ye may eat: the locust after his kind, and the beetle after his kind, and the grasshopper after his kind.

"These also shall be unclean unto you among the creeping things that creep upon the earth; the weasel, and the mouse, and the tortoise, and the ferret, the chameleon, and the lizard, and the snail, and the mole.

"And every creeping thing that creepeth upon the earth shall be an abomination; it shall not be eaten" (Leviticus 11).

Islamic and Jewish dietary laws are similar. Where there is no refrigeration or rapid transportation of foodstuffs, the importance of such laws is evident. Pork, which is frequently contaminated by worms, the Taenia Solium, and unless properly cooked, may be harmful.

Except for the Seventh Day Adventists, who follow the Muslim and Jewish food laws, Christians believe that clean, wholesome food has been prescribed by God. Seventh Day Adventists, in addition to following the Torah and Koran dietary laws, are vegetarians.

> *"Now the Spirit speaketh expressly, that in the latter times some shall depart from the faith, giving heed to seducing spirits, and doctrines of devils: Speaking lies in hypocrisy; having their conscience seared with a hot iron.*
>
> *"Forbidding to marry, and commanding to abstain from meats, which God hath created to be received with thanksgiving of them which believe and know the truth.*
>
> *"For every creature of God is good, and nothing to be refused, if it be received with thanksgiving; For it is sanctified by the word of God and Prayer"* (1 Timothy 4:1-5).

There is certainly nothing wrong with the dietary laws of some religions. It is important that foodstuffs should be carefully collected and prepared. Food spoils if not refrigerated, especially meat and fish.

When the Torah and Koran were written, nothing was known about cholera, E. coli, salmonella, and parasites. However, with modern refrigeration, hygiene, and preparation, former food laws are outmoded. Washing hands thoroughly after use of the toilet, boiling and cooking food to kill bacteria, or use of gamma or X-rays on food products to sterilize them, and pasteurization, have prevented the spread of diseases in modern times.

Disallowing infected food handlers to work in restaurants is important. The famous Typhoid Mary, who was responsible for spreading Typhoid to a number of families where she worked as a cook is a classical case of an epidemic due to improper hygiene.

MORMONISM AND THE WORD OF WISDOM

In February, 1823, the prophet Joseph Smith received a revelation, known as the Word of Wisdom, found in D&C 89:

1. "Inasmuch as any man drinketh wine or strong drink among you, behold it is not good. Strong drinks are not for the belly, but for the washing of our bodies."

2. "Tobacco is not for the body, neither for the belly, and is not good for man."

3. "Hot drinks are not good for man." This has been interpreted as caffeine and theobromine containing drinks such as coffee, tea, and colas.

4. "All wholesome herbs God hath ordained for the use of man. Every herb in the season thereof and every fruit in the season thereof."

5. "Yea, flesh also of beasts and of fowls of the air, I the Lord, have ordained for the use of man with thanksgiving; nevertheless they are to be used sparingly. They should not be used, only in times of winter, or of cold, or famine."

6. "All grain is ordained for the use of man and of beasts."

7. "All saints who remember to keep and do these saying shall receive health in their navels and marrow into their bones, and find wisdom and treasures of knowledge. And run and not be weary and walk and not faint. And I, the Lord, give them a promise, that the destroying angel shall pass by them,

as the children of Israel, and not slay them."

Although in the '50s when Alton Ochsner, a famous surgeon, claimed tobacco could cause cancer of the lung and was greeted with derision by fellow doctors, over the years research has proven the harmful effects of smoking and recently advertising of cigarettes on billboards and television has been curtailed.

The consumption of liquor has not yet reached the political heat that smoking has received, and alcohol continues to exact its awful human toll in destroyed lives and tremendous expense. Drinking under the influence kills and maimes thousands each year and should not be tolerated. Freedom should not be curtailed, but certainly the restriction of advertisement should be enacted and warning labels applied to alcoholic beverages, the most abused of all drugs, just as it is in the case of tobacco products.

Chapter 24

LAWS AND CUSTOMS

USURY AND OTHER FORBIDDEN PRACTICES

"We forbade the Jews wholesome things which were formerly allowed them, because time after time they have debarred others from the path of God, because they practice usury, although they were forbidden it—and cheat others of their possessions" (K 4:138).

"God has permitted trading and made usury unlawful. God has laid His curse on Usury and blessed almsgiving with increase. God bears no love for the impious and the sinful" (K 2:275).

"Who is guilty of Theft, cut off their hands. That is the punishment enjoined by God. But whoever repents and mends his ways, shall be pardoned by God" (K 5:35).

"Do not devour one another's property by unjust means, nor bribe the judges with it in order that you may wrongfully and knowingly usurp the possessions of other men" (K 2:188).

Islam follows the admonition of Christ, who said burning sacrifices is no longer acceptable: *"God does not demand sacrificial animals"* (K 5:101).

Although Shiism and Sunnism have been bitter rivals ever

since Muhammad, their fundamental beliefs are identical. The Koran does not allow for individual Islamic denominations:

> *"Have nothing to do with those who have split up their religion into sects"* (K 6:158).

> *"We will surely punish the schismatics, who have broken up the scriptures into separate parts, believing some and denying others"* (K 15:89).

PRAYER AND FASTING

> *"Those that fast and those that kneel and prostrate themselves; those that enjoin justice, forbid evil, and observe the commandments of God shall be richly recompensed"* (K 9:111).

> *"Evening, and morning, and at noon, will I pray"* (Psalms 55:17).

> *"He heareth the prayer of the righteous"* (Proverbs 15:29).

> *"And when thou prayest, thou shalt not be as the hypocrites are; for they love to pray standing in the synagogues and in the corners of the streets that they may be seen of men. Verily I say unto you, they have their reward. But thou, when thou prayest, enter into thy closet. . . Pray to thy Father which is in secret and thy Father which seeth in secret shall reward thee openly.*
> *"Use not vain repetitions, as the heathen do, for they think that they shall be heard for their much speaking.*
> *"Be not ye therefore like unto them; for your Father knoweth what things ye have need of, before ye ask him.*

"After this manner therefore pray ye:

"Our Father which art in heaven, Hallowed be thy name.

"Thy kingdom come. Thy will be done in earth, as it is in heaven.

"Give us this day our daily bread.

"And forgive us our debts, as we forgive our debtors.

"And lead us not into temptation, but deliver us from evil; For thine is the kingdom, and the power and the glory, for ever. Amen" (Matt. 6:4-13).

"Moreover when ye fast, be not, as the hypocrites, of a sad countenance . . . But unto thy Father, which seeth in secret, shall reward thee openly" (Matt. 6:17,18).

"Wherefore he that prayeth, whose spirit is contrite, the same is accepted of me if he obey mine ordinances" (D&C 52:15).

"Organize yourselves; prepare for every needful thing and establish a house of prayer, a house of fasting, a house of faith, a house of learning, a house of glory, a house of order, a house of God" (D&C 88:118).

The Koran teaches sharing wealth with the poor, as does the Torah and Bible: *"Tell my servants, those who are true believers, to give alms in public and in private"* (K 14:30).

"A kind word with forgiveness is better than charity followed by insult. God is self-sufficient and gracious. Believers, do not mar your almsgiving with taunts and mischief-making, like those who spend their wealth for the sake of ostentation and believe

neither in God nor in the Last Day. Those that give their wealth for the cause of God can be compared to a grain of corn which brings forth seven ears, each bearing a hundred grains" (K 2:260 and 263).

Jews and Christians also are to give to the poor and help the needy:

"If there be among you a poor man of one of thy brethren within any of the gates in thy land which the Lord thy God giveth thee, thou shalt not harden thine heart, nor shut thine hand from thy poor brother. But thou shalt open thine hand wide unto hIm, and shalt surely lend him sufficient for his need, in that which he wanteth . . . The Lord thy God shall bless thee in all thy works . . . For the poor shall never cease out of the land" (Deut. 15:7-11).

"Though I speak with the tongues of men and of angels, and have not charity, I am become as sounding brass, or a tinkling cymbal. And though I have the gift of prophecy . . . And all knowledge, and have not charity, I am nothing.

"And though I bestow all my goods to feed the poor . . . And have not charity (love) it profiteth me nothing. Charity suffereth long and is kind; charity envieth not; charity vaunteth not itself, is not puffed up.

"And now abideth faith, hope, charity, these three; but the greatest of these is charity" (1 Cor. 13).

"Wo unto yo rich men, that will not give your substance to the poor, for your riches will canker your souls.

"Wo unto you poor men, whose hearts are not broken, whose spirits are not contrite, and whose

bellies are not satisfied, and whose hands are not stayed from having hold upon other men's goods, whose eyes are full of greediness, and who will not labor with your own hands" (D&C 56:16,17).

MASTURBATION

A former cabinet member of the Clinton administration made the statement that masturbation is not only normal, but may be healthy physically and mentally. This flies in the face of Biblical reproof:

> *"Let not sin therefore reign in your mortal body, that ye should obey it in the lusts thereof. Neither yield your members as instruments of unrighteousness unto sin; but yield yourselves unto God, as those that are alive from the dead, and your members as instruments of righteousness under God. For sin shall not have dominion over you; for ye are not under the law, but under grace.*
>
> *"What then? Shall we sin, because we are not under the law, but under grace? God forbid. For the wages of sin is death; but the gift of God is eternal life through Jesus Christ our Lord"* (Romans 6:12,13,15,23).

SLAVERY AND EQUALITY

Islam allows slavery. *"God has given you wives from among yourselves and through your wives, sons and grand-children. He has provided you with good things. God has favored some among you above others. Those who are so favored will not allow their slaves an equal share in what they have. Would they deny God's goodness? On the one hand there is a helpless slave, the property of his master. On the other, a* man on whom We have bestowed Our bounty, so that he gives of it both in private and in public. Are the two equal? God forbid!" (K 16:68-73).

Mormons have always felt slavery was anathema to the teachings of God. A revelation was given to Joseph Smith at Kirtland, Ohio, December 16, 1822:

> "Therefore it is not right that any man should be in bondage one to another. For this purpose I have established the Constitution of this land, by the hands of wise men whom I raised up unto this very purpose, and redeemed the land by the shedding of blood" (D&C 101:79,80).

ADULTERY

> "You shall not commit adultery, for it is lewd and evil" (K 17:31).

> "The adulterer and the adulteress shall each be given a hundred lashes" (K 24:1).

> "Thou shalt not commit adultery" (Ex. 20:14).

> "If a man be found lying with a woman married to an husband, then they shall both of them die" (Deut. 22:22).

Adultery by Mormons is cause for excommunication, but forgiveness also is available: "He that has committed adultery and repents with all his heart and does not repeat the act is forgiven" (D&C 42:45).

Chapter 25

CREATION AND EVOLUTION

"You people! If you doubt the Resurrection remember that We created you from dust, then from a living germ, then from a clot of blood, then from a half formed lump of flesh. . . Then We bring you forth as an infant, then you grow up and reach your prime. Some die young, some live to an abject old age when all they knew they know no more" (K 22:1).

"It is He who has given you life and he who will cause you to die and make you live again" (K 22:64).

"Those whom you invoke besides God could never create a single fly through their combined forces" (K 22:71).

"God created every beast from water. God creates what he pleases" (K 24:41).

"God created you and He will then reclaim you. Some will have their lives prolonged to abject old age, when all they once knew they will know no more. All knowing is God and mighty" (K 16:68).

"We created man from dry clay, from black moulded loam, and before him Satan from smokeless fire" (K 15:19).

"Does man think We shall never put his bones together again? Indeed, We can remold his very fingers!" (K 75:1).

"And the Lord God formed man of the dust of the ground, and breathed into his nostrils the breath of life; and man became a living soul" (Gen. 2:7).

"People are ever learning and never able to come to a knowledge of the truth" (2 Tim. 3:7).

God created everything spiritually before He created it physically:

"I, the Lord God, made heaven and the earth, and every plant of the field before it was in the earth before it grew. For I, the Lord God, created all things spiritually, before they were naturally upon the face of the earth; for in heaven created I them; and there was not yet flesh upon the earth, neither in the water, neither in the air" (P. of G. P., Moses 3:4,5).

At the resurrection we will be given a new body, the exact duplication of the one we have in mortal life, beautifully perfect, and not subject to disease, deterioration, or pain. *"But even the very hairs of your head are numbered. Fear not therefore"* (Luke 12:7).

Devolution in which all living things may deteriorate is ubiquitous.

Alas, is the skeleton of Homo Erectus a grotesque dwarf,
An Achondroplast or pleomorph?
Or malformed before birth from AIDS or the syph,
Could the "missing link" be just a myth?
—Anonymous

Beginning with Adam and Eve, men and women had brilliant minds and magnificent bodies, living hundreds of years. However, it didn't take long after leaving the Garden of Eden and being cut off from direct contact with God to deteriorate mentally, spiritually, and physically.

Contrary to the Darwinian theory, animals and humans exposed to hostile environments do not evolve into stronger creatures; rather, just the opposite. They deteriorate. God made creatures for each environment.

People who fail to keep the laws of God become subject to Satan, war-like, full of hatred, vengeance, dictatorial, and animalistic.

The Law of Thermodynamics causes complex forms to deteriorate always into simpler forms, never the opposite.

"Evolutionists theorize that organisms develop into more complicated organisms, evolving into more sophisticated and complex strictures. This flies in the face of the law of thermodynamics with the well proved fact that complex forms constantly degrade into more simple forms" (Marvin Cook, *Science and Mormonism,* p. 236, Chapter XIV).

According to Hall: "Thus the large components such as DNA necessary to form life would be impossible to synthesize by chance" (Eyring, Henry the *Father*/a scientist, quoted by Cook, p. 253).

> Men say they know many things;
> But lo! They have taken wing—
> The arts and sciences,
> And a thousand appliances;
> The wind that blows
> Is all that anybody knows.
> —Thoreau

"And it came to pass that Moses called upon God, saying: 'Tell me, I pray thee, why these things are so, and by what thou madest them? And behold, the glory

of the Lord was upon Moses, so that Moses stood in the presence of God, and talked with him face to face, and the Lord God said unto Moses: For thine own purpose have I made these things.

"And by the word of my power have I created them, which is mine Only Begotten Son, who is full of grace and truth. And worlds without number have I created; and I also created them for mine own purpose; and by the Son I created them. Only an account of this earth and its inhabitants will I give to you. There are many worlds which have passed away by the word of my power, and there are many which now stand, and numberless are they unto man; but all things are numbered unto me; for they are mine, and I know them.

"As one earth shall pass away, even so another shall come, for there is no end to my works, neither to my words. For this is my work and my glory, to bring to pass the immortality and eternal life of man" (Moses 1).

Einstein, when asked about a haphazard origin of life answered, "God does not throw dice."

"By the unspeakable gift of the Holy Ghost, God will give every worthy man and woman knowledge, and nothing will be withheld—whether there be boundaries of the heaven, the moon, and the stars. God shall give people an understanding . . . According to that which was ordained by the Eternal God before the world was created" (D&C 121:26-31).

"Nothing offends God more and none is His wrath kindled against except those who do not accept His hand in all things" (D&C 59:21).

Chapter 26

THE KORAN, THE BIBLE, AND MORMONISM

Muhammad, who was supposedly unable to read or write—
"Therefore have faith in God and his unlettered Prophet" (K
7:158)—claimed he received the revelations of the Koran from
God via the angel Gabriel. As previously noted, much of the
Koran is similar to accounts in the Bible. The references to the
story of Moses and Abraham as well as Adam and Eve, Isaac,
Jacob, Noah, and other prophets are analogous.

Reference to the story of Moses in Exodus is mentioned
many times in the Koran. *"Remember how We delivered you
from Pharaoh's people, who had opposed you cruelly, slaying
your sons, and sparing only your daughters. Surely that was
a great trial for your Lord. We parted the sea for you and
taking you to sea drowned Pharaoh's men before your very
eyes"* (K 2:47).

On the other hand, the Koran embellishes references in the
Bible:

> *"Bear in mind the words of Moses to his people. He
> said, 'Remember my people, the favor which God has
> bestowed upon you. He has raised up prophets among
> you, made you kings and given you that which He has
> given no other nation. Enter, my people, the holy land
> God has assigned you. Do not turn back and lose all.*
>
> *"We have bestowed on them a Book which We*

imbued with knowledge, a guide and a blessing to true believers. On the day it is fulfilled, those that have forgotten it will say: 'Our Lord's apostles have surely preached the truth before.' We never charge a soul with more than it can bear. For those that have denied and scorned Our regulations the gates of heaven shall not be opened; nor shall they enter Paradise until the camel shall pass through the eye of a needle" (K 7:49 and 7:19).

The latter mimics Matthew 19:23: *"And again I (Jesus) say unto you, It is easier for a camel to go through the eye of a needle than for a rich man to enter into the kingdom of God."*

"The rich man's wealth is his strong city, and as an high wall in his own conceit" (Proverbs 18:11).

The Koran reflects the story of Lot and Sodom and Gomorrah: *"And Lot, who said to his people: 'Will you persist in these lewd acts which no other nation has committed before you? You lust after men instead of women. Truly, you are a degenerate people"* (K 7:26).

"We gave the Book to Moses, but differences rose about it, and but for a Word from your Lord, their fate would have been sealed" (K 11:104).

"Praise be to God who has revealed to His servant a Book shorn of contradictions" (K 18:1).

"God created you and He will then reclaim you. Some shall have their lives prolonged to abject old age, when all they once knew they shall know no more. All knowing is God, and mighty" (K 16:68).

ABRAHAM AND THE URIM AND THUMMIM

"I, Abraham, talked with the Lord, face to face, as one man talks with another, and He told me of the works which His hands had made. I had the Urim and Thummim which the Lord had given me, and saw the stars, including the great one, Kolob, which is near to the throne of God. And the Lord said unto me, by the Urim and Thummim, that Kolob was after the manner of the Lord—one revolution was a day unto the Lord, it being one thousand years compared to the earth" (Abraham 3:11,2,3,4).

"The Lord had shown unto me, Abraham, the intelligences that were organized before the world was, and among these were many of the noble and great ones. Abraham, you are one of them. You were chosen before you were born. Your name shall be great among all nations. These facts exist: there are two spirits, one being more intelligent than they; there shall be another more intelligent than the other; I am the Lord thy God, and I am more intelligent than all" (Abraham 3:19,22,23).

"I kept the records of my ancestors concerning the right of the Priesthood, and also a knowledge of the beginning of the creation, and also of the planets and the stars" (Abraham 1:31).

The diaspora of the Jews occurred as prophesied. Their resiliency in view of their persecution throughout history is remarkable and due to the fact that they are God's chosen people and the Lord will never forget His covenant with them.

THE JEWS BROUGHT SALVATION TO THE GENTILES

"Many of the Gentiles shall say: A Bible! A Bible! We have a Bible. And there cannot be any more Bible.

"But thus saith the Lord God: O fools, they shall have a Bible; and it shall proceed forth from the Jews, mine ancient covenant people. And what thank they the Jews for the Bible which they receive from them: Yea, what do the Gentiles mean? Do they remember the travails, and the labors, and the pains of the Jews, and their diligence unto me, in bringing forth salvation unto the Gentiles?

"O ye Gentiles, have ye remembered the Jews, mine ancient covenant people? Nay; but ye have cursed them, and have hated them, and have not sought to recover them. But behold, I will return all these things upon your own heads; for I the Lord have not forgotten my people" (2 Nephi 20:3-5).

THE LAW OF MOSES

The Law of Moses consists of the following decrees:

1. Eternal laws such as the Ten Commandments, which exist today and form the basic laws of civilized nations. The Commandments also include laws of moral behavior, which are immutable.

2. Laws having to do with crime, with death, imprisonment or monetary punishment.

3. Temporary laws such as animal sacrifice, walking a certain number of steps on the Sabbath, priestly activities such as burning incense and repetitive prayers and covering oneself with ashes. These were discontinued by Jesus Christ, who said in Him the law was fulfilled.

The Ten Commandments were embellished by zealous scribes:

1. If thou wilt make me an altar of stone thou shall not build it of hewn stone, for if thou lift up thy tool upon it, thou has polluted it.

2. Neither shalt thou go up by steps to mine altar, that thy nakedness be not discovered.

3. His master shall bore his ear with an awl and he shall serve him forever.

4. He that smiteth his father or his mother shall be surely put to death.

5. He that stealeth a man and selleth him shall surely be put to death.

6. He that curseth is father or mother shall be put to death.

7. Thou shalt give life for life, eye for an eye, tooth for a tooth, hand for a hand, foot for a foot, burning for burning.

8. If a man smite his servant or his maid with a rod and he lie under his hand, he shall be punished. Notwithstanding, if he continue a day or two he shall not be punished, for he is his money.

Only Jesus Christ, not Moses, could redeem men from their sins (Mosiah 16:6).

> *"Yet the Lord God saw that his people were a stiff-necked people, and he appointed unto them a law, even the law of Moses"* (B.O.M., Mosiah 3:14).

> *"By Him all that believe are forgiven from all their sins from which ye could not be forgiven by the Law of Moses"* (Acts 13:39).

> *"Having therefore obtained help of God, I continue unto this day . . . Saying none other things than those which the prophets and Moses say should come—that*

Christ should suffer and should be the first that rise from the dead and show light unto the Gentiles" (Acts 16:22).

JEWS, LIKE MUSLIMS, BELIEVE GOD WILL FIGHT FOR THEM

"The lord your God which goeth before you, He shall fight for you according to all that He did for you in Egypt before your eyes" (Deut. 1:30).

Moses was told that the Jews would be scattered: *"And the Lord shall scatter you among the nations . . . But if thou shalt seek the Lord thy God, thou shalt find him if thou seek him with all thy heart and soul. He will not forsake thee nor destroy thee, nor forget the covenant of thy fathers"* (Deut. 4:27)

Moses was also told that Christ would come: *"The Lord thy God will raise up unto thee a prophet from the midst of thy brethren. Like unto me, unto him ye will hearken"* (Deut. 18:15).

JEWS DON'T BELIEVE IN UNISEX

"The woman shall not wear that which pertaineth to a man; neither shall a man put on a woman's garment; for all that is an abomination unto the Lord thy God" (Deut. 22:5).

THE OLD TESTAMENT, LIKE THE KORAN TEACHES PREDESTINATION

"The Lord killeth and maketh alive; he bringeth down to the grave and he bringeth up; the Lord maketh the poor and maketh the rich" (1 Sam. 2:6).

The words of Job are very reassuring: *"Happy is the man whom God correcteth; therefore despise not chastening of the Almighty."*

"For I know that my Redeemer liveth and that He shall stand at the latter day upon the earth . . . And though after my skin worms destroy my body, yet in my flesh shall I see God" (Job 5:17 and 19:25).

"Which of the Lord's blessings would you deny?" (K 51:1-52. This is repeated 31 times. Similar to Psalms 136).

THE POTENTIAL GODHOOD OF MAN
IS REITERATED

"Thou shalt be perfect with the Lord thy God" (Deut. 18:13).

"Ye are gods; and you are children of the most high" (Psalms 82:6).

"Jesus answered them, Is it not written in your law, I said, ye are gods?" (John 10:34).

ISRAEL WILL REGAIN THE LAND OF
THEIR INHERITANCE

"But the Lord liveth, that brought up the children of Israel out of the land of Egypt . . . And I will bring them again into their land that I gave unto their fathers . . . And they shall dwell in their own land" (Jer. 16:14-16 and 23:5,8).

"For the law was given by Moses, but grace and truth came by Jesus Christ" (John 1:17).

"Search the scriptures, for in them ye think ye have eternal life; and they are they which testify of me" (John 5:39).

"For if ye had believed Moses, ye would have believed me, for he wrote of me" (John 5:46).

JESUS ADMONISHED THE JEWS TO KEEP THE COVENANTS

"Jesus saith to them, 'If ye were Abraham's children, ye would do the works of Abraham" (John 8:39).

JESUS WOULD TAKE THE GOSPEL TO OTHER LANDS

"Other sheep I have which are not of this fold; them also I must bring, and they shall hear my voice, and there shall be one fold, and one shepherd" (John 10:16).

THE PRIESTHOOD OF MELCHIZEDEK

Because of the wickedness of the Israelites in making gods out of gold and worshipping them while Moses was receiving the Ten Commandments, Moses broke the tablet on which the laws were written, and the priesthood of Aaron was taken from the people.

The higher priesthood of Melchizedek was restored during Christ's mortal life: *"Whither the forerunner of us entered, even Jesus, made an high priest forever after the order of Melchizedek"* (Heb. 6:20).

In the LDS Church there are two priesthoods, namely, the Melchizedek and Aaronic. The first is named such because Melchizedek was a great priest. Before his time it was called the Holy Priesthood, after the Order of the Son of God. But out of reverence to the name of the Supreme Being, and to avoid the too frequent repetition of His name, the church in ancient days called that priesthood the Melchizedek Priesthood.

The holders of this Priesthood possess the keys of all the spiritual blessings of the church. They have the privilege of receiving the mysteries of the kingdom of heaven, and to enjoy the communion and presence of God the Father and Jesus (D&C 107:64-98).

On the Mount of Transfiguration Jesus, Moses, and John the Baptist (Elias) gave the higher priesthood to Peter, James, and John. In turn, these keys were given by the presidency of the ancient church to Joseph Smith and Oliver Cowdery on August 12, 1830: *"Listen to the voice of Jesus Christ, your Lord, your God, and your Redeemer; And also with Peter, James, and John, whom I have sent to you to be apostles and special witnesses of my name and bear the keys of your ministry"* (D&C 27:12).

"The Priesthood of the Son of God is the law by which worlds are created, were, and will continue forever and ever. It is the system which brings worlds into existence, and peoples them, gives them their revolutions, their days, weeks, months, years, seasons and times. It is a perfect system of government and ordinances" (JD of Brigham Young quoted by John A. Widtsoe, 1941).

THE ANTI-CHRISTS

"Whosoever denieth the Son, the same hath not the Father, but he that aknowledgeth the Son hath the Father also. Who is a liar but he that denieth that Jesus is the Christ? He is an anti-Christ that denieth the Father and the Son" (1 John 2:22,23).

"But notwithstanding the law of Moses, they did look forward to the coming of Christ, considering that the law of Moses was a type of his coming, and believing that they must keep those outward performances until the time that he should be revealed unto them. Now they did not suppose that salvation came by the law of Moses; but the law of Moses did serve to strengthen their faith in Christ . . . Relying upon the spirit of prophecy, which spake of those things to come" (Alma 15:15,16).

Only in America where freedom was established could the Gospel of Jesus Christ be restored.

FREEDOM IS A GOD-GIVEN RIGHT

"Wherefore the Lord gave unto man that he should act for himself. "Adam fell that men might be and men are that they might have joy. The Messiah cometh that He may redeem the children of men from the fall. Because they are redeemed from the fall they have become free forever, knowing good from evil . . . They are free to chose liberty and eternal life through the great atonement or to choose captivity and death according to the captivity and power of the devil, for he seeketh that all men might be miserable like unto himself.

"Do not choose eternal death according to the will of the flesh and evil which is therein which giveth the spirit of the devil power to captivate and bring you down to hell that he may reign over you in his own kingdom" (2 Nephi 2:16,25,27,29).

THE PROPHET JOSEPH SMITH IS PREDICTED

"Yea, Joseph truly said, thus sayeth the Lord to me: 'A seer will I raise up . . .And his name shall be called after me, and it shall be the name of his father, and the fruit of thy loins shall write and also that which shall abe written by the fruit of the loins of Judah shall go together into the confounding of false doctrines . . . And bring them to the knowledge of their fathers in the latter days and also to the knowledge of my covenants." (2 Nephi 3:11,12).

AMERICA IS A LAND CHOICE ABOVE ALL OTHER LANDS

"Thus saith the Lord, 'I will fortify this land against all other nations. He that fighteth against Zion shall perish. This land shall be a land of liberty unto the Gentiles, and their shall be no kings upon the land.

"For it is choice above all other lands" (2 Nephi 2:10-13).

"For it is wisdom in the Father they should establish in this land and set up as a free people be the power of the Father that these things might come forth from them unto the remnant of your seed, and that the covenant of the Father may be fulfilled" (3 Nephi 21:4).

ISAIAH WAS OFTEN QUOTED BY CHRIST

The book of Isaiah is the only complete book found among the lost scrolls. Two thirds of Isaiah is quoted in the Book of Mormon.

"Because the words of Isaiah are not plain unto you, nevertheless they are plain to those who are filled with the spirit of prophesy" (2 Nephi 25:4).

"We talk of Christ, we rejoice in Christ, we preach of Christ, and write according to our prophesies, that our children may know to what source they may look for the remission of their sins" (2 Nephi 35:26).

Isaiah predicts the revelation of the Book of Mormon to one who is not learned in the 29th chapter. This is reiterated in the year between 559 and 545 B.C.: *"The Lord God will deliver again the book and the words thereof to him that is not learned.;and the man that is not learned shall say: I am not learned. Then shall the Lord Say unto him: The learned shall not read them, for they have rejected them., and I am able to do mine own work; wherefore thou shalt read the words which I shall give unto thee. I am God; and I am a God of miracles, and I will show unto the world that I am the same yesterday, today, and forever, and I work not among the children of men save it be according to their faith. Forasmuch as this people draw near unto me with their mouth and with their lips do honor me, but have removed their hearts far from me . . . Therefore, I will proceed to do a marvelous work among the people, yea, a marvelous work and a wonder, for the wisdom of their wise and learned shall perish"* (2 Nephi 27:19-26).

"Remember that I spake unto you and said that when the words of Isaiah should be fulfilled—behold they are written. Ye have them before you, therefore search them. And they shall believe me that I am Jesus Christ, the Son of God. Then shall the Father gather

them together again and give unto them Jerusalem for their inheritance" (3 Nephi 20:11,31,33).

Joseph Smith was given the Book of Mormon, which was written in Egyptian on gold plates, which he was able to translate by means of a device called the Urim and Thummim, which is mentioned in the Torah, and is similar to the famous Rosetta Stone, found by Napoleon, which was used to decipher ancient Egyptian.

"If we could have written in Hebrew, behold ye would have had no imperfections in our record" (Mormon 9:33).

CONTENTION AMONG CHURCHES IS PREDICTED

In order to overcome death and meet the demands of justice for the sins of mankind, it was necessary for the Son of God to experience mortal life, overcome death and atone for the sins of the world. Jehovah chose Jerusalem because the House of Israel were His chosen people. However, *"There is no other nation on the earth that would crucify their God"* (2 Nephi 10:3).

"Behold, my soul delighteth in proving unto my people the truth of the coming of Christ for this end hath the law of Moses been given" (2 Nephi 11:4).

"It shall come to pass that the churches which are built up, and not unto the Lord, where one will say, Behold, I, I am the Lord's and the others will say I, I am the Lord's. And they shall contend one with another and their priests shall contend one with

another and they shall teach with their learning and deny the Holy Ghost. . . They do err because they are taught by the precepts of men . . . Otherwise the learned and the rich are puffed up in their hearts and teach false doctrine" (2 Nephi 28:3,4).

"For this intent we keep the Law of Moses, even as it was accounted unto Abraham unto the commandments of God in offering up his son Isaac, which is a similitude of God and His only Begotten Son" (Jacob 2:26,27).

BE NOT OVERBEARING

There are many wonderful people in the world, and many churches, (except the church of the devil) teach part of the truth. However, the Church of Jesus Christ is the only true church on the earth.

"And after having received the record of the Nephites, yea, even my servant Joseph Smith, Junior, might have power to translate through the mercy of God, by the power of God, the Book of Mormon, and also those to whom these commandments were given, might have power to lay the foundation of this church, and bring it forth out of obscurity and out of darkness, the only true and living church upon the face of the earth, *with which I the lord am well pleased, speaking unto the church collectively and not individually—for I the lord cannot look upon sin with the least degree of allowance; nevertheless, he that repents and does the commandments of the lord shall be forgiven.*

"For I am no respecter of persons, and will that all men shall know that the day speedily cometh; the hour is not yet, but is nigh at hand, when peace shall be taken from the earth and the devil shall have power over his own dominion" (D&C 1).

"The Book of Mormon, which contains the truth and the word of God—which is my word to the Gentile, that soon it may go to the Jew, of whom the Lamanites (American Indians) are a remnant, that they may receive the gospel, and look not for a Messiah to come who has already come" (D&C 19:26, 27).

"See that ye are not lifted up in pride, and do not boast of your wisdom and strength . . . Use boldness, but not overbearing" (Alma 38:12).

Christ redefined the Law of Moses, changing hatred to love, urging men and women to overcome passions of the flesh and become like Him.

"Old things are done away,and all things have become new. Therefore I would that ye should be perfect, even as I, or your Father who is in Heaven is perfect" (3 Nephi 47, 48).

THE BOOK OF MORMON IS INCOMPLETE

"And now there cannot be written in this book even a hundredth part of the things which Jesus did truly teach unto the people. Behold, I was about to write them, all of which were engraved upon the plates of Nephi, but the Lord forbade it, saying, 'I will try the

faith of my people" (3 Nephi 26:6,11. Additional scriptures will eventually be forthcoming).

DENY NOT CONTINUED REVELATION
AND PROPHESY

"Wo unto them that shall deny the revelations of the Lord and say the Lord no longer worketh by revelation or by prophesy, or by the gifts or by tongues, or by healings, or by the power of the Holy Ghost!" (3 Nephi 29).

Do not people today need revelation by God just as in ancient times?

THE JEWS SHALL NOT BE SPURNED

"Yea, and ye need not any longer hiss, nor spurn, nor make game of the Jews, nor any of the remnant of the house of Israel; for behold, the Lord remembereth his covenant unto them, and he will do unto them according to that which he hath sworn" (3 Nephi 29:8).

WRITTEN RECORDS ARE ESSENTIAL

"For it was not possible that our father Lehi could have remembered all these things . . . except it were for the help of these plates; for he, having been taught in the language of the Egyptians (while still in Jerusalem) therefore, he could read these engravings. Were it not for the things which have been preserved by the hand of God, we would have been like the

Lamanites, who know nothing of these things, or do not believe them when things are taught because of the traditions of their fathers, (by word of mouth), which are not correct" (Mosiah 1:4,5).

THE FATHER AND THE SON

Jesus Christ is known as both the Father and the Son. He acquired the title Father because He created this earth under the direction of God the Father, and thus became the father of this earth. He is the Son of God because He was begotten by the Father in the flesh.

"Being the Father because He was conceived by the power of God, and the Son because of the flesh" (Mosiah 15:2,3).

LITTLE CHILDREN DO NOT NEED BAPTISM

"He that supposeth that little children need baptism is in the gall of bitterness. For awful is the wickedness to suppose that God saveth one child because of baptism and the other must perish because he hath no baptism" (Moroni 2:14,15).

"There are records which contain much of my gospel which have been kept back because of the wickedness of the people" (D&C 6:26).

WHOEVER DENIES FREEDOM IS EVIL

"That law of the land which is constitutional, supporting the principle of freedom and maintaining

rights and principles belongs to all mankind and is justifiable before me. I the Lord God, make you free— and whatsoever more or less than this cometh of evil.

"According to the laws and Constitution of the people, which I have suffered to be established—that every man may act in doctrine and principle according to the moral agency I have given him, that every man shall be accountable for his own sins; therefore it is not right that any man should be in bondage one to another. For this purpose have I established the Constitution of the land, by hands of wise men whom I raised up unto this very purpose and redeemed the land by the shedding of blood" (D&C 101:77-80).

The Koran states that Christ was not seen after he was crucified and resurrected, but the true history is irrefutable. *"That He was seen by Cephas, then of the twelve, then by over 500 at once; then James and the other apostles, and last by me (Paul) also"* (1 Cor. 15:5,6,7).

In ancient America at the time of the crucifixion there were tempests and earthquakes and darkness, attesting to the crucifixion of Christ. The people gathered in the land called Bountiful heard a voice, saying, *"Behold my Beloved Son, in whom I am well pleased,in whom I have glorified my name— hear ye him."*

Christ appeared to the people and said, *"Behold, I am the light and life of the world. I have drunk out of that bitter cup which the Father hath given me, and have glorified the Father in taking upon me the sins of the world . . . I came unto my own, and my own received me not. "And the scriptures concerning my coming are fulfilled. I am Alpha and Omega, the beginning and the end"* (3 Nephi 11:11, & 9:16,18).

Jesus then taught the people the Beatitudes—His teachings

take precedence over the law of Moses, taught the Lord's prayer, taught the Gospel, and that He would not manifest himself except by the Holy Ghost.

Chapter 27

JEHOVAH IS JESUS CHRIST

"And God spoke unto Moses and said unto him, I am the Lord. And I appeared unto Abraham, unto Isaac, and unto Jacob, by the name of God Almighty, but my name, Jehovah, was I not known to them" (Exodus 6:3).

The Old Testament has been called the greatest collection of literature and revelations known to man. The coming of Jesus was foretold by Adam, Moses, David, Zechariah, and especially Isaiah. The Book of Mormon prophets including Alma, King Benjamin, Samuel and others also prophesied the birth and mission of Christ Jehovah on this earth.

"Behold the days come, saith the lord that I will raise unto David a righteous branch , a King shall reign and prosper, and shall create judgment and justice in the earth. In his days Judah shall be saved, and Israel shall dwell safely. And this is his name whereby he shall be called, THE LORD OUR RIGHT-EOUSNESS" (Jer. 23:5,6).

"And after the house of Israel should be scattered they should be gathered together, or, in fine, after the Gentiles had received the fullness of the Gospel . . . The House of Israel should be gathered in, or come to the knowledge of the true Messiah, their Lord and their Redeemer" (1 Nephi 14).

*"And Moses said unto God, Behold, when I come
unto the children of israel and shall say unto them,
'The God of your fathers hath sent me unto you; and
they shall say to me, What is his name? What shall I
say unto them?*

*"And God said unto moses, I AM. THAT I AM. Thus
thou say unto the children of Israel, I AM hath sent me
unto you"* (Exodus 3:13,14).

When Jesus went to the Mount of Olives in Jerusalem, He
revealed his true identity to a group of Jews by saying, 'Your
father Abraham rejoiced to see my day; and he saw it, and was
glad.

*"Then said the Jews unto him, thou art not yet fifty
years old and hast thou seen Abraham?*

*"Jesus said unto them, Verily, verily, I say unto
you, Before Abraham was I Am"* (John 8:56-58).

This was the same as Jesus' saying, "I AM THE GREAT
JEHOVAH.

The Jews were so angry at Christ that they took up rocks to
stone Him to death.

Jesus affirmed that he was Jehovah, the God of Israel, the
God of Moses and the ancient prophets in a revelation to
Joseph Smith the Prophet, at Fayette, New York, in September,
1830: *"Listen to the voice of Jesus Christ, your Redeemer, the
GREAT I AM, whose arm of mercy hath atoned for your sins"*
(D&C 29:1).

After His resurrection, Jesus walked with two of His disci-
ples, and sat and ate with them. Their eyes were opened, and
they knew him. Jesus had said to them: *"O fools, and slow of
heart to believe all that the prophets have spoken: Ought not*

Christ to have suffered these things, and to enter into his glory?

"And beginning at Moses and all the prophets, He expounded unto them in all the scriptures the things concerning himself" (Luke 24:25,26,27, and 30,31).

"And ye shall know that I am the Lord, when I have opened your graves O my people and brought you out of your graves, and shall put my spirit in you and ye shall live" (Jer. 44:25).

"And ye shall know the truth and the truth shall make you free" (Luke 8:52).

"We saw the Lord and his voice was. . . the voice of Jehovah, saying: I am the first and the last; I am He who liveth. I am He who was slain; I am your advocate with the Father" (D&C 110:3,4).

THE JEWS, THE CHOSEN PEOPLE, DID NOT RECOGNIZE JESUS

"The angel of the Lord spake unto me saying: Behold, saith the Lamb of God, after I have visited the remnant of the house of Israel—and this remnant of whom I speak is the seed of thy father—wherefore, after I have visited them in judgment and smitten them by the hand of the Gentiles, and after the Gentiles do stumble exceedingly, because of the most plain and precious parts of the gospel of the Lamb which have been kept back by that abominable church . . . I will be merciful unto the Gentiles in that day, insomuch that I will bring forth much of my gospel, which is plain and precious . . . They shall write many things which I shall

*minister unto them, which shall be plain and precious
. . . These things shall be hid up, to come forth unto the
Gentiles, by the gift and the power of the Lamb . . . And
in them shall be written my gospel"* (1 Nephi
13:34,35,36).

The personal appearance on earth to Joseph Smith by God
the Father and His Son Jesus clearly identify the Father and
His Son Jesus appeared to the people of ancient America as
recorded in the Book of Mormon and He then summarized the
law:

> *"The covenant which I have made with my people
> is not all fulfilled. But the law which was given unto
> Moses has an end in me. Behold, I am the law and the
> light. This is the law and the prophets, for they truly
> testified of me"* (3 Nephi 15).

> *"I came unto my own, and my own received me
> not. The Scriptures concerning my coming are
> fulfilled. I am in the Father and the Father in me. In me
> hath the Father glorified his name. In me is the law of
> Moses fulfilled. You shall offer up no more the shed-
> ding of blood; your sacrifices and burnt offerings are
> done away. You shall offer as a sacrifice a broken
> heart and a contrite spirit. I have come to save the
> world from sin. Whoever repents and comes unto me
> as a little child, will I receive, for such is the kingdom
> of God. I have laid down my life, and have taken it up
> again. Therefore, repent and come unto me ye ends of
> the earth and be saved"* (3 Nephi 9:16-22).

> *"Behold, I am Jesus Christ whom the prophets
> testified should come unto the world. I am the light and
> life of the world. I have drunk out of that bitter cup*

which the Father has given me and have glorified the Father in taking upon me the sins of the world. Arise and come to me and thrust your hands into my side and feel the prints of the nails on my hands and feet, that you may know that I am the God of Israel, and the God of the whole earth and I have been slain for the sins of the world" (3 Nephi 11:10-14).

"I am the Lord thy God, the Holy One of Israel, thy Saviour. I, even I am the Lord and besides me there is no Saviour" (Isaiah 43:10, 46:5,6).

ALL PEOPLE WILL KNOW THAT JESUS IS JEHOVAH

"All flesh shall know that I the Lord am your Saviour, the mighty one of Jacob" (Isaiah 51:3).

"I am the God of Israel, and the God of the whole earth, and have been slain for the sins of the world" (3 Nephi 11:44).

"Not one tittle hath passed away from the law, but in me it hath been fulfilled" (3 Nephi 12:18).

"Behold, I am He that gave the Law and I am He who covenanted with my people Israel" (3 Nephi 15:5).

Christ was the Son of God. He was Jehovah of the Old Testament, the God of Israel. He was with the Father in the beginning and came to earth to experience mortal life, overcome death, and atone for men's sin.

CHRIST JEHOVAH HELPED IN THE CREATION

"Behold, I am Jesus Christ the Son of God. I created the heavens and the earth. I was with the Father from

the beginning. I came unto my own, but they received me not. In me is the Law of Moses fulfilled" (3 Nephi 9:15,17).

CHRIST JEHOVAH'S MESSAGE TO ALL MUSLIMS AND JEWS

Abraham is the patriarch of three monotheistic faiths— Judaism, Christianity, and Islam. Fifteen million are Jews, two billion are Christians, and 1.2 billion are Muslims.

> "Now the Lord had said unto Abram, 'Get thee out of thy country . . . And I will make of thee a great nation, and I will bless thee, and make thy name great; and thou shalt be a blessing. And I will bless them that bless thee and curse him that curseth thee; and in thee shall all families of the earth be blessed.'
>
> "And the Lord appeared to Abram, and said, Unto thy seed will I give this land. And I will make thy seed as the dust of the earth . . . So that if a man can number the dust of the earth, then shall thy seed also be numbered.
>
> "And Melchizedek , the priest of the most high God . . . Blessed him: 'Blessed be Abram of the most high God, possessor of heaven and earth.'
>
> "And God appeared to Abram . . . And said: Be thou perfect. And I will make my covenant between me and thee . . . Thy name shall be Abraham, for a father of many nations have I made thee" (Gen. 12:1,2,3; Gen. 13:16; Gen. 14:18,19 & Gen. 17:1,2,3).

Abraham's name appears in 25 of the 114 chapters of the Koran.

As previously noted, the Koran recognizes Abraham, Ishmael, Isaac, Jacob, Moses and Jesus as prophets. *"All these We (God) exalted above the nations. . . On these men We bestowed the Scriptures, wisdom and prophethood"* (K 6:80-88).

> *"And tell of Our servants Abraham, Isaac, and Jacob . . . And of Ishmael and Elisha, who were all just men, of might and vision whom . . . made We made pure with the thought of the hereafter"* (K 38:44).

Chapter 28

ISLAM vs. MORMONISM

ISLAM	MORMONISM
God is a spirit	God is a man with body parts and passions.
Christ was the son of Mary	Christ is the Only Begotten Son.
Christ was just another prophet	Christ created this earth under the direction of God the Father
Christ was not crucified	Christ was crucified, overcame death and atoned for the sins of the world.
There is only one God	God the Father and God the Son appeared to Joseph Smith in 1820
God has no consort	There is a Mother in Heaven
Heaven is for the righteous men to lie on couches with voluptuous virgins	As man is God once was. As God is, man may become.

ISLAM	MORMONISM
Polygamy is acceptable	Polygamy was acceptable only for a brief period. It is an abomination by God and is no longer permitted.
Alcohol and gambling not permitted	Alcohol is not permitted. Gambling is an evil habit.
No Pork or seafood without scales	All meat and vegetables are provided by God, but sparingly
	Tobacco use not allowed
Women are inferior to men	Women are equal to men. They are to be loved, educated, cared for, and exalted.
Abortion allowed	Abortion allowed only to save mother's life, or rape or incest
"An eye for an eye"	"Love thy neighbor as thyself."
Make war in the name of God	Bloodshed may be indicated to defend yourself and family.
The Koran is the only true Book	The Bible is the word of God as long as it is translated correctly.
Adultery is a sin	Adultery is a sin. It may be forgiven if repented.

ISLAM	MORMONISM
Homosexuality is degenerate	Homosexuality is a sin
There are Seven Heavens	All people shall be resurrected because of the Atonement of Christ. There are three degrees of glory, the Telestial, Terrestrial, and Celestial.
The Koran is incongruous and full of fallacies	The Book of Mormon is the word of God interpreted by Joseph Smith by the use of the Urim and Thummim through the Holy Ghost.
Muhammad was the last prophet	Joseph Smith was a prophet of God and the church is led by a prophet today under the direction of Jesus Christ.
No further revelation	Revelation is continuous.
No baptism	Baptism by immersion is required.
Divorce is by a statement	Eternal marriage in temples. Baptism as well as other ordinances for the dead are done by proxy.

ISLAM	MORMONISM
Islam by force	Conversion by persua--sion
Muhammad was the founder of Islam	Muhammad of history is not the same Muhammad beloved by his Muslims. His followers fought battles with the Koran in one hand and the sword in the other. Joseph Smith was the prophet of God, who said a prophet is not always a prophet. He interpreted the Book of Mormon, a history of ancient Americans who were visited by the resurrected Christ and given the true Gospel.
America is Satanic	America was founded by God. The Constitution came under the direction of God. If its people are righteous, their God-given freedoms will never be lost

Chapter 29

FREEDOM AT RISK

America and all democracies are at war. The threat of militant Muslims today to destroy the freedoms of people in the world is just as big a threat as Nazism, Stalinism, and Fascism were in the last century. But, now the perpetrators invoke the name of God to justify their Satanic evil.

The Koran teaches many good things: A loving and merciful God; the contribution of prophets of the Old Testament as well as Jesus; the giving of alms to the poor; forgiveness and kindness. It repeats the story of Adam, Noah, Moses, Abraham, Isaac, Ishmael, Lot, Jacob, Joseph, and other prophets of the Old Testament.

The Koran teaches high moral conduct, preaches against adultery, homosexuality, and theft, and like the Torah and traditions of the Jews, It upholds the Ten Commandments as given by God to Moses.

The Koran when spoken in Arabic has beautiful verses which bring people to tears. On the other hand, much of the Koran is for medieval days, not applicable to modern times. A large part of it, like part of the Old Testament, deals with animal sacrifice and stifling, severe laws concerning everyday life.

Islam teaches belief in one God, but the Koran constantly uses the plural We to describe the words of Allah. The Koran degrades women, calls them inferior to men, tells men that women are their fields and to constantly plow them. Women are to veil themselves and cover their bodies. In strictly ruled countries like Afghanistan under the Taliban, women were denied education, people were forbidden to watch television, or play music.

PARTS OF THE KORAN ARE ABSURD NONSENSE

The Koran is ludicrous when it describes Heaven as a place where worthy men will forever live in mansions by streams of running water, lying on silk-lined couches with voluptuous virgins, and served delicious drinks by young boys.

Unfortunately, Islam militants use the Koran to justify their Jihad, *"An eye for an eye, a tooth for a tooth, an ear for an ear,"* copying the ancient scriptures of the Torah, which preceded the Koran by a thousand years, and which both Jews and Muslims need to overcome if peace is ever to come to the world.

Despite the fact that the Koran recognizes Jesus as a prophet—His teachings of forgiveness, love of enemy, doing good to those that spitefully use you, turning the other cheek, giving one's cloak also to one who sues you for your coat—all the admonitions taught by Christ are ignored.

Although the Koran teaches tolerance and "some Christians and Jews are good people," countries such as Indochina, Saudi Arabia, Libya, Algeria, Pakistan, Yemen, Kuwait, Syria, Iraq, Sudan, and Iran, which are governed by Islamic law, do not allow other religions, and have theocratic, non-democratic governments. Christians and Jews are being massacred in some Muslim-controlled countries.

Until our defeat of the Taliban in Afghanistan, that country had imposed stifling restrictions on the activities and customs of its people. Unfortunately, the temporary government intends to rule by Islamic law and only time will tell if a moderate regime, allowing some freedoms of its people will ensue.

Muslims as well as Jews need to remember the last part of this verse: "We decreed for them a life for a life, an eye for an eye, a nose for a nose, an ear for an ear, a tooth for a tooth, a wound for a wound. *But if a man charitably forbears from retaliation, his remission shall atone for him*" (K 5:44).

Esposito suggests that Islam needs to accept change just as its sister traditions, Judaism and Christianity (Exposito, John. *The Islamic Threat, Myth or Reality*. N.Y. 1995).

Fazlur Rahman, in his book, *Islam and Modernity* emphasizes that Muslims need new leaders who can reinterpret Islamic law and recognize the separation of state and religion is necessary in a modern world.

Professor Sardan of King Abdul Aziz University of Jedah, concerning the negative role of the fundamentalists: "By emphasizing in the mechanics of prayer and absolution, length of beard, and mode of dress, the dynamic nature of many Islam injunctions and the creativity and innovation that Islam fosters within its framework, they have founded intolerant, compulsive and tyrannical orders and provided legitimacy to despotic nepotic political system of government. They have closed and constricted many inquiring minds by their unending quibble over semantics. They have divorced themselves from human needs and conditions. No wonder that the majority of Muslims today pay little attention to them and even foster hostility toward them."

Rufig Zaharia, in his book (*The Struggle Within Islam*, London, 1998), reminds Muslims that it was leaders such as Ataturk of Turkey, who abolished the Caliphate, Jennah of Pakistan, Nassar and Sadat of Egypt, who recognized that some changes were necessary, and their secular outlook assured equality for the future of billions of Muslims all over the world.

Many blacks in America have joined Islam to fulfill a protest against the sins of America. Islam seems to offer a spiritual expression they do not find in Christianity or Judaism.

When Truman recognized Israel, in May 1948, immediately after Ben Gurian declared Israel a nation, Arab Americans regarded this as a betrayal. In response, Truman said: "I'm sorry, but I have to answer to hundreds of thousands who are anxious for the success of Zionism. I do not have hundreds of thousands of Arabs among my constituents (Public papers of the U.S. Government. Printing office, 1958). The right of Israel, the only democratic country in the Middle East, to exist as a nation has been threatened since its inception. Terrorist groups such as the Hamas in Palestine, the Wahhabis in Egypt and Saudi Arabia, the Hizballah in Iran, Holy Warriors in the Philippines and Chechnya, and radical Muslims in Indonesia, the Sudan, Nigeria, Algeria, and almost every other country in the world have a common goal: the destruction of democracy and the establishment of Islam to dominate and rule the world. We now know there are over 10,000 trained Al Qaeda members in the United States.

Islamic Jihad has obtained funds in America under the guise of charitable organizations.

There are 100,000 Muslim students enrolled in American universities and colleges. There are 6,000 Muslim doctors in America and 600 mosques. Steven Emerson has noted in his recent book, *American Jihad*, that the Holy War of radical Muslims has attempted to invade American colleges, most notably, the University of Southern Florida. Many courageous American Muslims have denounced militant Muslim extremists, often at great risk. Only a small number of American Muslims are militantly anti-America, pro Jihad.

America has been the most charitable country on earth. After the defeat of Germany and Japan, we forgave those countries, gave billions to them to restore their nations, and defended them from a takeover by atheistic communism.

Those who depict America as just a country represented by Satanic movies, music, television, and literature filled with violence, adultery, nudity, drunkenness, and drugs, make a great mistake.

The majority of Americans are decent, law-abiding people who believe in God, have close loving families, and will not allow anyone to destroy their freedoms—freedom of the press, freedom to vote, freedom to assemble, freedom to bear arms, freedom to become educated, freedom to invent, freedom to develop new ideas, new companies, freedom to fail, freedom to defend their families with their blood, freedom to choose the religion of their choice. Yes, we have our faults, but in God we trust, and God will be our guide, and God will keep us free.

Americans and our allies dropped thousands of tons to the people of Afghanistan while we were destroying the evil grip of the Taliban and Al Qaeda on their country. We have proven that Muslims are not our enemy, but if they attempt to destroy democracy and freedom, which are God-given rights, which Americans have fought and died for, we will fight and and we will triumph.

Muslims worldwide need to abolish the dictate of part of the Koran which fosters war and the spread of Islam by force under the will of God. They need to uphold that part of the Koran which teaches forgiveness, lack of revenge, tolerance for people of other religion. They need to emphasize the good parts of the Koran concerning righteousness, faith, giving to the poor, and love of their fellowmen.

We are in the struggle of good versus evil—the final battle between the forces of Satan and Christ, the battle which began in Heaven when God the Father chose Christ the First Born, over Satan, Son of the Morning. Christ advocated freedom of choice, while Satan would allow no such freedom. Forgiveness was anathema to Lucifer, the Prince of Darkness.

God the Father chose Christ's plan, providing prophets to instruct people, and finally giving His only Begotten Son to overcome death and atone for the sins of mankind. Freedom is the corner stone of the Gospel of Jesus Christ.

Men and women were given the opportunity to attain perfection and godhood by following the Commandments of God, and by living Christ-like lives, with love ultimately overcoming hate; peace overcoming war; democracy overcoming dictatorship, good overcoming evil.

Freedom will win. Love will win over hate. Good will win over evil.

The Spread of Islam

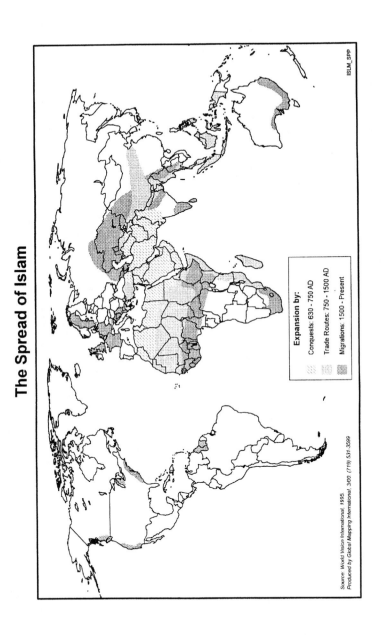

Expansion by:

Conquests: 630 - 750 AD

Trade Routes: 750 - 1500 AD

Migrations: 1500 - Present

Source: *World Vision International, 1995.*
Produced by Global Mapping International, 300, (719) 531-3599

ISLM_SPP

142

Islam is Spreading Rapidly - Growing in Many Nations

Muslim Growth Rate

75 to 1495 (Fast)
40 to 74 (Medium)
1 to 39 (Slow)
-100 to 0 (Negligible or Negative)

Note: Percent growth rate over 10 year period, 1990-2000. Countries less than
.1 percent Muslim have been included in the Negligible category.
Derived from 1990-2000 religion growth figures, Patrick Johnstone, Operation World, 1993.
Produced by Global Mapping International, 3/00, (719) 531-3599

ISLM_GRP

143

BIBLIOGRAPHY

Ahmed, Akbar S. *Discovering Islam*. London, 1988.

Al Furqua. *Historical Atlas of Religions in the World*. 1975.

Arnold, Thomas W. *The Caliphate*. London 1965.

   The Preachings of Islam. London,1975.

McEvedy, ed. *Atlas of World Population History*.

Bat Yeor. *The Decline of Christianity Under Islam From Jihad to Dhimminitude, 20th Century*. London 1996.

Holy Bible, Authorized King James Version, Book of Mormon, Doctrine and Covenants, Pearl of Great Price. Church of Jesus Christ of Latter-day Saints. 1986.

Bendiner, Elmer. *The Rise and Fall of Paradise*. New York, 1983.

Cook, Melvin and Cook, Garfield. *Science and Mormonism*. Deseret News Press, 1967.

Dawood, N.J. Translator. *The Koran*. Penguin Books. 1999.

Douay-Confraternity. *The Holy Bible*. P. J. Kennedy and Sons, 1950.

Dozy, Reinhart. *Spanish Islam*. London, 1913.

Emerson, Steven. *American Jihad*. The Terrorists Living Among Us. The Free Press, 2002.

Evans, John Henry. *Joseph Smith, An American Prophet*. The Macmillan Company, 1933.

Esposito, John L. Editor. *The Oxford History of Islam*. Oxford University Press, 1999.

   The Islamic Threat, Myth or Reality. New York. 1995.

Eyring, Henry. *The Faith of a Scientist*. Bookcraft. 1967.

Fregosi, Paul. *Jihad*. Prometheus Books. Amherst, New York. 1998.

Grunebaum, G. Von. *Classical Islam , A History, 600-1258*. London, 1958.

Medieval Islam: A Study In Cultural Orientation. Chicago,1947.

Guillalaume, Alfred. *Islam*. Oxford, 1990.

Haddad, Yvonne Y. *Muslims of America*. Oxford University Press. 1991.

Hall, J. *Thermodynamics And Kinetics of Spontaneous Generation*. Nature. 186:693-94. 1960.

Hutchinson, Paul. *The World's Great Religions*. Time, Incorporated. 1957.

Jessee, Dean C. *Writings of Joseph Smith*. Deseret Book Co. 1984.

Johnson, Paul. *A History of the Jews*. New York. Harper and Row, 1987.

Keegan, John A. *History of Warfare*. London, 1984.

Leyden. *The Encyclopedia of Islam*. London, 1913, and 1960.

MacKay, Calvin R. *Jehovah is Jesus Christ*. M.C. Printing, 1995.

MacKay, Calvin R. *The Compleat Mormon*. M.C. Printing. 1991.

Mayr, Ernst. *Semantics and the Origin of Species*. Columbia University Press, 1982.

Malloup, Amen and Rothschild. *The Crusades Through Arab Eyes*. 1987

Moojan, Momen. *An Introduction to Shi'I Islam. The History and doctrine of Twelve Shi' Ism*. George Ronald Oxford. 1985.

Nibley, Hugh. *Islam and Mormonism—A Comparison*. Ensign 2 March 1072.

O. Bierne, Kate. Martyred. *Muslim murder and mayhem against Christians*. National Review/December 3, 2001.

Palmer, Spencer J., ed. *Mormons and Muslims; Spiritual*

Foundations and Modern Manifestations. Religious Studies Center, Brigham Young University, 1983.

Peters, Rudolph. *Jihad, Medieval and Modern.* Leiden, 1977.

Islam and Colonialism. The Hague, 1979.

Peterson, Daniel. *Abraham Divided.* Aspen Books, 1992.

Pipes, Daniel. *Understanding Islam in Politics.* 1983.

Robinson, Stephen E. *Are Mormons Christians?* Bookcraft, 1991.

Rushdie, Salman. *The Satanic Verses.* London, 1988.

Ruthvin, Malise. *Islam in the World.* London, 1984.

A Satanic Affair: Salman Rushdie and the Rage of Islam. London, 1990.

Shakir, M.H. Translator. *The Quar'an.* Tarsile Quar'an, Inc. 2001.

Watt, W. Montgomery. *Concerning the Constitution of Medina-Muhammad at Medina.* Oxford, 1956.

Wells, H. G. *The Outline of History.* London, 1858.

Williams, John A. *Islam.* George Braziller. 1962.

Wright, Robin. *Sacred Pages. The Crusades of Modern Islam.* London, 1986.

Zaukaria, Rafiq. *The Struggle Within Islam.* London, 1988.

Zebiri, Kate. *Muslims and Christians Face to Face.* Oxford, 1997.

Zwener Institute of Muslim Studies. Altadera, California, 1987.

INDEX

About the Author

C. Reynolds MacKay and his wife Virginia live in Provo, Utah. He graduated from the University of Utah and the University of Utah Medical School.